"Frances Frei and Anne Morriss are the real deal and offer a fresh, new take on the most important leadership challenges of our time: making big change happen, building organizations where everyone can rise, and solving hard problems when the clock is ticking . . . loudly."

—**TYRA BANKS**, supermodel turned entrepreneur; founder, SMiZE & DREAM

"This hands-on playbook shows readers how to accelerate change and transform organizations while also nurturing a culture of trust, inclusivity, and collaborative problem-solving. It's an essential resource for any leader looking for the inspiration and tools to lead their team to new levels of excellence."

—**KATHLEEN HOGAN**, Executive Vice President and Chief Human Resources Officer, Microsoft

"In *Move Fast & Fix Things*, Frei and Morriss have given us a masterpiece on trust, leadership, and business. This is required reading for anyone who wants to build audacious, high-performance cultures."

—**BILL MCDERMOTT**, Chairman and CEO, ServiceNow

"Speed wins, but only if you pair it with strategy, trust, and respect for everyone on the court. Frei and Morriss have generously shared the road map for how to move fast while also excelling as teams and organizations."

—**NADIA RAWLINSON**, Operating Chairman, Chicago Sky (WNBA)

"*Move Fast & Fix Things* invites us into a conversation all leaders should be having: how to create the conditions where people can truly, sustainably thrive."

—**BECKY SCHMITT**, Executive Vice President and Chief People Officer, PepsiCo

"Frances Frei and Anne Morriss have produced a fun, super-practical, step-by-step guide to leading lasting change at speed."

—**HUBERT JOLY**, senior lecturer, Harvard Business School; former Chairman and CEO, Best Buy; and author, *The Heart of Business*

"With *Move Fast & Fix Things*, Frei and Morriss have done the unthinkable: they've written a book that will make you look forward to Mondays."

—**MEENA HARRIS**, founder and CEO, Phenomenal Media

"The Frei/Morriss team has delivered again! *Move Fast & Fix Things* is a remarkable, insightful book that will help you accelerate change inside your organization while simultaneously building trust and unleashing the potential of your people. I highly recommend this leadership masterpiece."

—**STEPHEN M. R. COVEY**, bestselling author, *The Speed of Trust*

"Frei and Morriss have rewritten the playbook for change. Toss out The 8 Steps, forget the 7-S Framework, and get ready to discover the fastest path to renewing your organization. With a clear plan for how to spend your Monday through Friday, they make it easy to keep it all straight. But what matters most is that you start *today*. Full of engaging stories and unexpected insight, *Move Fast & Fix Things* will not disappoint the growing number of fans of this amazing duo."

—**AMY C. EDMONDSON**, Novartis Professor of Leadership and Management, Harvard Business School; author, *Right Kind of Wrong*

"Frei and Morriss are masters of positive organizational change, and *Move Fast & Fix Things* is a practical guide to doing just that. It's hard to find accessible, easy-to-apply advice on leading change, and I couldn't recommend the book more. A great companion to *Unleashed*."

—**CLAIRE HUGHES JOHNSON**, former Chief Operating Officer and current Corporate Officer and Adviser, Stripe

"Frei and Morriss's values of 'trust' and 'moving fast' are critical in any thriving environment. Their advice is invaluable to anyone trying to make an impact at work."

—**MARC LORE**, serial entrepreneur; founder, Chairman, and CEO, Wonder

"*Move Fast & Fix Things* unlocks the secret to leading change that lasts without sacrificing speed. This revolutionary guide equips leaders with the tools to solve their toughest problems, create a high-performance culture, and communicate powerfully—all while maintaining an exhilarating speed."

—**SARAH PFUHL**, New York–based Global General Counsel for Litigation, Regulatory Enforcement, and Investigations

"Frei and Morriss have a habit of blowing your mind with the most strategic insights while giving you practical, tangible ideas you can use in tomorrow's staff meeting. I give this book to everyone in my life who's trying to build organizations that will not only endure but also flourish and prosper in a future defined by speed, uncertainty, and limitless possibility."

—**DARA TRESEDER**, Chief Marketing Officer, Autodesk

MOVE FAST
& FIX THINGS

Frances Frei and Anne Morriss

MOVE FAST & FIX THINGS

THE TRUSTED LEADER'S
GUIDE TO SOLVING
HARD PROBLEMS

HARVARD BUSINESS REVIEW PRESS
BOSTON, MASSACHUSETTS

Cataloging-in-Publication data is forthcoming.

ISBN: 978-1-64782-287-3

eISBN: 978-1-64782-288-0

The paper used in this publication meets the requirements of the American National Standard for Permanence of Paper for Publications and Documents in Libraries and Archives Z39.48-1992.

For Alec and Ben, again and always:
May you be patient with love
and impatient with progress.

"What if I fall?"
Oh, but my darling,
"What if you fly?*"*

—Erin Hanson

CONTENTS

PREFACE

We are not here to tell you that you or your company are some-how broken. But we are here to meet our readers where they are in their experience of trying to make things better, and the start-ing point for most adventures in organizational change is that "something around here needs to be *fixed*."

A cornerstone of our work is that leadership is the practice of imperfect humans leading imperfect humans. If you accept this as a reasonable starting point, then it follows that any collection of us builds imperfect organizations. In this book, we're inviting you to get curious about those imperfections. Only when we drag our fingers along the floorboards of our experiences, only when we go in search of where good intentions have fallen short, only then can we begin the work of making things better. As we reveal in the pages ahead, we find this to be a deeply optimistic pursuit.

We're also inviting you to be impatient with progress. We designed this book to be a fast, fun guide to solving hard prob-lems and accelerating the pace of change. It's a playbook that's designed to free up the resources that make problems solvable—things like energy, creativity, even joy. These are things that can feel difficult to access right now, as we all try to live, and to lead, through historic levels of uncertainty. And yet without them, we have little chance of thriving.

We hope that you read the book, of course, but we also hope that you *do* it—that you test, apply, and improve these ideas in your own lives and workplaces. Our ambition is to have your back along the way. We want to stand next to you on the rockiest, most exhilarating part of the leadership path, the part where you turn hopes and dreams into making a difference in the lives of other people.

In our last book, *Unleashed*, we introduced a new model for leadership based on the principle of empowering others not as a stylistic choice, but as the foundation of your success as a leader. In this book we show you how to apply the full force of empowerment leadership and achieve results in record time. Our biggest fans will even recognize some of the stories and examples from *Unleashed*, which we revisit here from a different, more practical angle. If we may be so bold, we suggest you read both books, in whichever order suits you.

In pursuit of this book's mission, we're aware that we're standing on the shoulders of the change leadership scholars who have deeply influenced us, both in their work and commitment to impact: giants like Rosabeth Moss Kanter, John Kotter, Mike Tushman, and Linda Hill. They have much to teach all of us, and you should devour their work, as we have, with gratitude and more-than-occasional awe. We are joining a conversation they so profoundly advanced because decades, centuries, and even millennia into the study of leadership, we still learn new things every day.

It's our privilege, once again, to share these insights with you.

MOVE FAST
& FIX THINGS

TRUST US, IT'S FIXABLE

S peed has gotten a bad name in business, much of it deserved. When Meta (née Facebook) printed "Move fast and break things" on cheerful company posters, it became the most visible convert of a widely held belief that we can either make progress or take care of people, one or the other. A certain amount of wreckage is the price we have to pay for inventing the future.

We've spent much of the last decade helping companies clean up that wreckage, and one of the main lessons from our work is that the trade-off at the heart of this worldview is false. The most effective leaders solve problems at an accelerated pace, while also taking responsibility for the success and well-being of their customers, employees, and shareholders.

They move fast and *fix* things.

How do they do it? In short, they invest as much time and energy into building trust—and, yes, sometimes rebuilding it—as they do into building speed. Speed unleashes your organization's energy and reveals where you're going. Trust convinces your stakeholders to come along for the ride. Think about whatever you're building as a plane taking off for a new destination: no one's getting on board without confidence in the aircraft, and without enough speed, you're not even getting airborne.

A Memorable Story That Illustrates the Themes of This Book

In a typical business book, we'd pause at this point for an aspirational-yet-accessible anecdote that brings our point to life, something with some drama to get and keep your attention. We will fulfill this implicit contract in the chapters ahead, which are filled with resonant stories and examples. But since we're not great at typical and this book is about *you*, we're going to first invite you to reflect on your own experience of speed and trust.

See figure I-1 for what we call our *FIX map*, our take on the requirements for *fast, iterative excellence* (see what we did there?). The map lays out the four potential trajectories of your company: Accelerating Excellence, Responsible Stewardship, Reckless Disruption, and Inevitable Decline. At first glance, where on this framework would you put your own organization? Are you moving fast or slow? Are you building or losing trust with your most important stakeholders? Don't overthink it; just pick one of the four quadrants. For extra credit, draw both axes on a blank sheet of paper and place yourself at a single point.

FIGURE I-1

FIX map

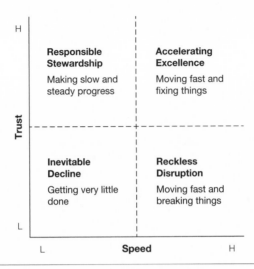

Here's our prediction based on having this conversation with countless leaders: a handful of you are already in Accelerating Excellence. You're creating high and rising value for your stakeholders, including your employees. You and your colleagues are creative and energized when you come to work without taking your eye off the achievement prize. If this describes your organization, then we'll simply congratulate you. Give this book to someone else or read on for our best advice on how to stay here (or for affirmation of your good instincts and choices).

But if we may be direct—another bad habit of ours—that's unlikely to be you. You're more likely to be in Responsible Stewardship or Reckless Disruption, either off the frontier of your potential impact or inflicting too much collateral damage as you sprint toward your goals. And you may even be in Inevitable Decline, without the advantage of *either* trust or speed. Figure I-2 will help you figure out where you are right now.

FIGURE I-2

Which quadrant best describes your organization?

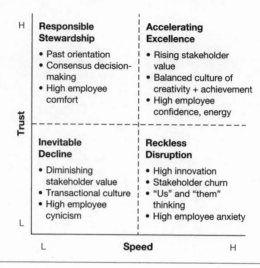

Now reflect on an organizational moment when the trade-off of being in one of these quadrants was clear to you, when you felt the cost on some visceral level. For those of you in Responsible Stewardship, it may have felt like process fatigue or the unwanted exit of talented colleagues. If you're in Reckless Disruption, it may have felt like anxiety in response to unmet client needs. Finally, if you're in Inevitable Decline, it may have just felt bad to go into work, which had become a ritual infused with frustration and cynicism.*

What was the cost of the moment you're recalling? To your team? To your customers? To *you*? And what if you or someone else had acted with urgency to strengthen the relationships at

---

*Keep the faith. This is not a state humans like to stay in for long, which means you have the clearest change mandate on the map.

the center of it? What would have happened next? How would this story, *your* story, have played out differently? These are the questions that animate this book.

Now let's begin where every good change story begins: with how you're choosing to spend your time.

A Playbook for Fixing Things Fast

We've had the privilege of advising thousands of leaders at all layers of a hierarchy—top, middle, bottom—as they've done the mostly unglamorous work of changing things. We've waded out into the murky middle of allegedly flat and matrixed organizations, where possibility was tough to find in all that matrixing. We've joined after-hours culture change teams as they looked for footholds of progress in organizations weighed down by a sticky past and a cynical view of the future.

We observed a clear pattern among leaders who were most effective at fixing things fast, the ones who fought their way to Accelerating Excellence. At a foundational level, these leaders had a distinct relationship with speed and trust. They treated pace and momentum as mission critical, and they also focused relentlessly on gaining and keeping the trust of their stakeholders. They experienced all the same things that hold the rest of us back, the same fears and doubts, but they believed that the antidote to those fears and doubts was fast, trust-building action.

As we pushed on *how* these leaders were able to break through, the relationship between trust and speed came into sharper focus for us. Not only were trust and speed foundational to their leadership impact, but there was also a clear relationship between them. The more trust these leaders earned—in both their own leadership and the organizations they were building—the faster they were able to change things in truly enduring ways. Trust was the cultural architecture on which their accelerated pace was built.

What emerged from this research is a playbook for fixing problems quickly, whether it's a broken company culture or a product that no longer fits seamlessly with your market. Layered on top of good general leadership hygiene, this playbook offers an order of operations for solving hard problems with the level of urgency they demand. We've organized the book according to this playbook—one step for each day of the week—and this is the work we're going to do together in the pages ahead:

1. ***Monday: Identify your real problem.*** You'll start by surfacing the roadblocks to progress, which may not be clear to you or be problems you know how to solve yet.

2. ***Tuesday: Solve for trust.*** Once you have confidence that you're addressing the right problem, you'll design a trust-building solution to it by running smart experiments and learning quickly.

3. ***Wednesday: Make new friends.*** Your next move will be to improve your emerging plan by tapping into other people's knowledge, focusing first on people who think differently than you do.

4. ***Thursday: Tell a good story.*** Now that you have conviction in your plan, it's time to tell a persuasive change story that connects the organization's past, present, and future.

5. *Friday: Go as fast as you can.* Finally, you'll empower everyone around you to execute the plan at an accelerated pace—and at a reduced risk of breaking things.

In the chapters ahead, we'll show you how to follow this playbook in your own organization on a fast cycle time of one step per "day." We'll start the week where you're starting, with some intuition around what needs to be fixed. We'll then create a viable plan for change and make it even better by embracing the value of difference. We'll craft a powerful change narrative, one that will unlock the energy and imagination of the people around you, and finally turn all this momentum into fast impact. If we do our jobs correctly, you won't just have a road map to Accelerating Excellence, you'll also be well on your way, cruising down that road at an exhilarating speed.

As you step on the gas, windows down and radio up, we're going to hold up our end of the deal and work to convince you that this is indeed the playbook that will make the difference for you. We're not asking you to believe us just yet (we've indulged ourselves with another two hundred pages to get all the way there), but we do hope you're willing to hear us out and keep reading. In keeping with the form, we'll lay out the most persuasive research and tell stories about change leaders and the companies they transformed. But as we've already revealed, the evidence we care *most* about is the change you're going to create in your own workplace. We're going to show-not-tell you we're on to something here by helping you move fast and fix your own organization.

Our goal is to give you a playbook for fixing any hard problem quickly, wherever you surface it inside your organization. This is another content departure from most management books (and from the other books we've written). Most resources you'll find are focused on solving a functional problem: how to retool your strategy, for example, or uncertainty-proof your supply chain. But the truth is, we don't know the type of problem that's holding you back, and you may not either. What we *do* know is that your problem is fixable, likely on a much shorter timeline than you think.

By the time you end the "week," your company will be moving at the pace that its real problems demand, while becoming an organization that's trusted at the *systems* level.

Just like personal trust, we've found that organizational trust relies on the presence of authenticity, empathy, and logic.[1] Just like personal trust, organizations that are losing trust—or failing to build as much trust as they could—tend to get shaky or *wobble* on one of these three dimensions.

We'll explore these ideas in more depth on Tuesday, but we'll offer this as a preview: the bad news about trust wobbles is that every organization has one at some point in its history. The good news about trust wobbles is that they're highly fixable with the right mindset and openness to learning. The thesis of this book is that by following our playbook, you'll be able to identify and fix your company's wobbles, unlock your organization's full potential, and go faster and farther than you ever dreamed possible.

How to Read This Book

We wrote this to help you build trust, solve problems, and accelerate change—all at the same time. It's meant to be an action-packed adventure in making rapid progress. In the pages ahead,

we'll challenge you to find out what happens when you identify and solve your real problems and reject the tentative, foot-
dragging pace of change that often masquerades as prudence but
is typically just *slow*.

If the pattern holds, it's not just your organization that will be
different by the end of this book—you'll be different, too. You'll
be more effective at the core task of leadership, which is to create
the conditions for other people to thrive. You'll be able to build
and rebuild trust at the organizational level, and you'll be able to
create possibility that other people believe in because they experience it as a change in their own reality, not as a theoretical idea
in your theoretical vision. You'll become the kind of leader the
best people want to work for because they become even better
when they're around you.

We're inviting you to join us on a condensed timeline of
activities to remove the most intractable barriers to excellence.
It's an exercise that's designed to free up the resources that make
companies fixable—things like optimism, imagination, and joy.
In the chapters ahead, we're playfully pointing out that you can
make significant progress in a single week, sometimes even in
a single day of focused work. This structure is meant to be fun
and fast and embody the core messages of the book: operate with
urgency, be wildly ambitious, fix as much as you can along the
way. And while the work of change is sometimes deadly serious,
you can avoid the trap of taking *yourself* seriously.

In truth, you're unlikely to measure the change you're leading in days. Most of you will take weeks and months to do this
work, which is perfectly reasonable. What we don't want you to
do is take *years*. Many leaders drag these kinds of activities out

over a year or more, getting themselves stuck on the runway in a variation of Responsible Stewardship that doesn't make strategic sense for their organizations. They choose slow-and-steady at precisely the moment when they need to jump-start their company's metabolism. Others skip over critical trust-building steps in the name of urgency, only to slow themselves down later when they have no choice but to circle back and clean up the mess. Our challenge to you is to defy these patterns by moving fast while *also* taking care of yourself, your colleagues, and your stakeholders.

We're also going to challenge you to shed the anxiety and self-distraction that can get in the way of Accelerating Excellence. When Frances was helping to lead an ambitious culture change effort at Harvard Business School—a campaign to make the school a more inclusive place for women—a well-meaning colleague pulled her aside before a high-stakes presentation and whispered, "You'd better be good." In his defense, he'd been getting pummeled by critics for months, but what she needed to hear in that moment was a reminder of the bigger truth of change leadership: yes, it's important to get the message right (see Thursday), but the fastest way to mess up change leadership is to make it about you. Your most important job right now is not to be good; it's to make sure that the people around you have a shot at being great.

Yes, the stakes of change are real—as real as they get for some of you, who are fighting for your company's or community's future—but the version of you who's going to make a difference isn't so worried about getting the audience's approval or looking like a leader or controlling future events. The version of you who's going to change things is a loose, free, present-tense-dwelling creature who doesn't know what's going to happen (how could you know?) but believes that change is important enough to go for it anyway.

We spend our time helping leaders to change and evolve. No one has ever said to us, "I wish I had taken longer and done less." What we do hear, again and again, is the opposite. If you decide to read on and join us on this quest, then you'll practice taking less time to do more of the things that will make your relationships, teams, and organizations stronger. Your mission is not to fix everything (although you'll fix a whole lot, in ways that may surprise and delight you). Instead, your mission is to convince yourself and the people around you that *everything is fixable*, that you can come together and solve the next hard problem that begins to hold you back with its seductive and mesmerizing complexity. It's to adopt the change leader's conviction that the moment that matters most is *now*.

Are You in the Right Place?

A quick disclaimer before we get started: this book is for anyone who wants to change things. It helps if you already have some formal influence over some part of an organization, but please stick around if you're good at managing up or aspire to a bigger leadership platform. We want to talk to you, too (and you may be more powerful than you realize).

We want to talk to all leaders, current and future, who are frustrated with the status quo and think there's a better way than "the way things are done around here." It's a conversation about evolution—fast evolution—but not revolution. If your instinct is to burn it all down because you see no reason to hope, then we might suggest other titles. We are shameless optimists who think that our best days as the planet's most collaborative species are ahead of us.

If cynicism is a go-to emotion right now, then we suggest coming back to this book when you're in a better place. You may have come by your disillusion honestly, but change leadership asks you to be in touch with your own agency and ability to influence your surroundings. It asks you to know your own power so that, among other things, you can introduce other people to theirs. If you're not feeling it, for whatever reason, then you won't be able to pull this off. And if you *are* feeling it, we'd like to offer some additional encouragement that you're right where you should be.

Move Fast Together

In the IPO prospectus Facebook filed in 2012, CEO Mark Zuckerberg explained the logic behind the company's commitment to "Move fast and break things." He wrote, "Moving fast enables us to build things and learn faster. However, as most companies grow, they slow down too much because they're more afraid of making mistakes than they are of losing opportunities by moving too slowly."[2] We agree with his observation, but as we hope to convince you in the pages that follow, those aren't your only two choices. You can build and learn quickly while *also* avoiding costly mistakes.

Zuckerberg himself seems to have come around to this world-view. In 2022, ten years after taking the company public, he announced that the company—now named Meta—would be moving fast *together*, operating with urgency while also "taking care of our company and each other."* For the record, we applaud this shift and are encouraged by it. And we invite you into this conversation because this kind of pivot should not take ten years. In fact, the timeline should be a whole lot closer to a week than a decade.

So what are you doing Monday?

---

*In 2014, Facebook swapped out the "break things" part for "with stable infrastructure," as in, "Move fast with stable infrastructure," a motto that, um, never quite caught on.

MONDAY

Identify Your Real Problem

The founding CEO of a local tech darling here in Boston made a habit of asking people on the front lines of his fast-growing company, "What would you do if you had my job?" The practice signaled the CEO's respect for his team and comfort in his own leadership skin. It also revealed cracks in the business he often wasn't seeing on his own. Whatever he thought he knew about his company, he learned it was never the full story.

Welcome to Monday, both a metaphor and—like the rest of this book—a suggestion we're making in good faith. You could wait for a more sentimental moment to begin your adventure in organizational change, such as the start of the year or the annual partners' meeting. Or you could receive the gift of renewal that comes around every seven days, also known as Monday.

Monday's ambition is to find the *problem*, a gritty little word we often dilute and defang in the American workplace, replacing it with more palatable substitutes like *issue* or *opportunity*. We like *problem* because it carries a sense of urgency. Inaction in the face of an issue or opportunity can be tolerated by polite society. A problem demands our attention.

Today we're going to invite you and a team of problem hunters to move fast and figure out what needs to be fixed. You're likely to have some idea of what that is already, and for some of you, that confidence will be well placed. You may be fighting a metaphorical fire—frustrated employees or an ascendant competitor—and it may seem like a relatively simple step to identify the source of the flames. We're still going to push you to go on this ride. Monday is about challenging the assumptions and storylines that have kept the organization from Accelerating Excellence. If the pattern holds, some of the stories you're holding on to most tightly (we're a meritocracy!) may not be quite as true as you think they are.

Those of you in Reckless Disruption are likely to discover that you've lost the trust of at least some stakeholders (if you're in Inevitable Decline, you can round *some* up to *all*). Those of you in Responsible Stewardship may realize that the company's metabolic rate is too low to sustain its ambition. These larger patterns have shown up in some way as "problems," which is what you're confronting today.

Today we're inviting you to focus on activities that will help you identify the most significant barrier to your organization's success. Along the way, we want you to begin to practice what it feels like to move fast and fix things simultaneously. Monday is

MONDAY'S AGENDA

1. Choose curiosity.

2. Build a team of problem solvers.

3. Explore what's holding you back.

4. Pick a candidate problem to solve.

5. Collect the organization's problem data.

6. Build a case with the data you have.

7. Learn more about your problem.

8. Decide what you're going to fix this week.

Materials You'll Need for Today

- Curiosity

- Comfort with discomfort

- Clear, transmissible understanding of your organization's strategy

- Easy access to organizational data

- Five to twelve colleagues with distinct roles and perspectives*

- One data analyst

- High-quality snacks

*The Agile purists, bless you, will argue that the optimal size of a temporary, cross-functional team like this is between five and eleven people. We simply can't, in good faith, endorse a number as awkward as eleven, particularly when it's so close to gorgeous number twelve.

also your first chance to make it clear to yourself and your colleagues that existing conditions are no longer acceptable. Tomorrow, on your watch, is going to be better than today.

Choose Curiosity

The most important item on your packing list today is curiosity. Our colleague Francesca Gino has made a rigorous case for the transformative impact of curiosity in the workplace, including its capacity to reduce errors, drive innovation, lower conflict, improve communication, and generally juice performance.[1] We suggest that you bring curiosity with you whenever practical, but it's a must-have item on Monday. Think of curiosity as a free, abundant, and renewable resource that dramatically increases your chances of seeing things clearly.

To be curious sounds easy enough, but here's the thing: curiosity and judgment don't play well together. In fact, as Gino has found, they essentially *can't coexist*. The first step to being curious for most of us, then, is to let go of judgment, to ask the judgy part of us to step aside for the day and summon the wide-eyed, uncynical part to take its place—the inner scientist on a mission to discover what's real and true about the world. It may have been a while since you let this part take the wheel (we feel safer when judgment is driving), so take a minute to get comfortable with curiosity's new status.*

*We are hereby invoking Dr. Richard "Dick" Schwartz's theory of the "multiple mind," known as Internal Family Systems. In our work coaching leaders, we sometimes refer to him as "Uncle Dick," as in, "Here's what we think Uncle Dick might say about this . . . " Dick, if you're alarmed by this, give us a call.

In our work with organizations in flux, we find it's sometimes harder for leaders to stop judging themselves than to stop judging the people around them. One leader we worked with had such a fierce inner critic that we gave the critic her own name ("Donna") and started referring to her playfully in the third person, as in, "Donna isn't invited to the next meeting." Donna was fine with other people not having all the answers, but she demanded flawless, omnipotent performance from this leader, which made looking for problems a high-risk proposition.

We'll go ahead and give you and your own version of Donna the tough news up front, so we can get this out of the way: your organization isn't perfect, and you probably had some role in its imperfection. You may have focused on things you like to do rather than need to do, or accepted mediocrity to avoid conflict, or hired too many people who are like you, habits of comfort rather than strategy. These things make you human, a condition you'll need to forgive yourself for. What matters now is your willingness to look without blinking and do something about what you find.

> **GUT CHECK:** Proceed when you're deeply curious
> about what you might discover today.

Build a Team of Problem Solvers

As you launch your search for the right problem to solve, we invite you to build a provisional team that can help you see the organization more clearly. This team is going to be gathering information from still *more* people, and so a healthy percentage of its members should be good at observing and honoring the experiences of others. They should be skilled, empathetic listeners who are comfortable in their own skin and aren't skittish in the presence of other people's emotions. They should *not* be overly impressed by you or your high-status colleagues.

In our work, we call these people *empathy anchors* (they reveal empathy even in the most stressful conditions), and their ability to read the room will be invaluable today. Gather a critical mass of empathy anchors and then fill out the rest of the team in ways that make sense for you, which probably means adding functional and demographic diversity. If you're missing women or younger employees or product people, and so forth, then balance it out. You'll be more likely to achieve Monday's mission—and any other mission—with people who don't all think the same way or have similar perspectives on the business, a pattern we're going to explore in more depth together later in the week.

When Michele Buck, CEO of Hershey's, began her campaign to transform the business into a "snacking powerhouse," a savagely competitive part of the American food budget (we prefer snacks to meals here in America), she pulled together a temporary team of people to help focus and fuel her ambition. Buck's selection criteria included comfort with change and risk, which did not conveniently line up with her most senior people. "Most people don't love change," Buck explained. "They don't love the idea of big transformation and taking big risks because obviously there can be a downside. . . . I looked across the organization, and I saw people who had shown evidence of . . . being able to see the future and see where trends were headed, to really think about what some of our greatest strengths were as a company and how we might fully leverage them."[2]

Buck built a nine-person team of mixed titles and levels who helped her to not only diagnose problems but also eventually solve them. And despite the blurriness of the group's decision rights, Buck ensured that the company "listened to their thinking . . . because I think a lot of times those really disruptive thinkers can get shut down."[3] She ultimately paired these disruptors with outstanding operators to ensure that ideas turned into projects and ultimately into transformative change, the sequence we're going to follow over the course of this book.

As you recruit your own internal team of innovative and empathetic thinkers, make a draft list of team members and then picture everyone together, having potentially tough conversations about what's *really* true, what's *really* happening in the organization, where the business is *really* going (or not going) without a significant change in vision or strategy or behavior. As our friend Lauren Collins Scott, executive design director at the iconic design firm IDEO, likes to say, "Look around the room and ask, 'Who is missing?' Do the folks at the decision-making table reflect the broader organization and consumer base?" This is a good time to practice building teams of talented people *whom you don't already know,* a leadership muscle that's underdeveloped for most of us.*

Finally, teams need names, so pick one that sounds career-enhancing and energy-producing. One team we worked with

---

*By "don't already know," we mean people who don't share your same networks, influences, and experiences. Here's a test: if you technically don't know someone, but they'd be very comfortable at your next house party, then your work is not done.

called this group the "Culture Strike Team," which hit the right notes. Another chose the "Forum" to add some intrigue and gravitas to the exercise. The idea is to spark interest, if not excitement, when the invitation shows up in your recruits' inboxes. Think less corporate speak, more excellent adventure. You get extra points for creating possibility by challenging your organization's unspoken language norms.

> **GUT CHECK:** Proceed when you've built a team of problem solvers and given yourselves a name that's worthy of your mission.

Explore What's Holding You Back

When nineteenth-century French novelist Marcel Proust (allegedly) drafted his famous questionnaire, the conceit of the exercise was to come up with a list of questions so powerful that they would reveal the respondent's true nature. Conversation had grown stale in the elite sitting rooms Proust frequented, and his questions were designed to make his friends more interesting. They included enduring, fan-favorite conversational prompts such as "What is the trait you most deplore in yourself?"

We now invite you to have a Proustian conversation with your colleagues that helps you uncover your organization's own true nature. In practical terms, the goal of this gathering is to draft a list of problems that need to be fixed. You may be tempted to do things that feel more "leaderly" at this stage—things like hiring fancy consultants to give you *their* opinion—but we promise you that the fastest, most effective way to identify problems is

FIGURE 1-1

Monday morning questions

People

- What do people like *most* and *least* about working here?

- Describe the characteristics of the person who is most likely to succeed at this company.

- What are the emotions you observe most frequently in your colleagues?

- When good people leave us, what are some common reasons? Are there patterns?

Strategy

- Who are our best customers? Why do they choose us instead of our competitors?

- When we lose good customers, what are some common reasons? Are there patterns?

- Which opportunities are we most effectively pursuing? Are we *under*-pursuing or neglecting any important opportunities?

- Which threats to the business are we most effectively addressing? Are we *under*-addressing or neglecting any important threats?

- What do our suppliers like *most* and *least* about working with us?

- Are we doing anything as an organization that can't be justified based on the expected return?

Capabilities

- What kinds of problems are we good at solving as an organization? Which are we *not* good at solving?

- When do our systems and processes reliably do and *not* do what we want?

- Is there anything we should be better at doing as an organization? Are there things we should know how to do that we don't?

Culture

- How does our culture set people up to succeed in their roles?

- Does our culture ever get in the way of our people's success? If so, in what ways?

- Which attitudes or behaviors should be adopted more widely?

- How would you describe our culture to someone outside the organization?

by having a skilled, direct, and unfiltered conversation with the people who are experiencing them.

Figure 1-1 is a sample list of "Monday morning" questions you can use as a starting place for this conversation. We offer this list for creative inspiration but encourage you to enthusiastically adapt it to your own organizational context. The goal here is to make everything discussable—even those parts of the business you think are going well—and surface any assumptions that may be parading around as facts. It's to pivot your own leadership mindset from advocacy to inquiry, as Chris Argyris, the great organizational behavioralist, described it.*

The questions you end up using should reflect your own reality as an organization. When Cinnabon's president Kat Cole was turning the company around, questions she asked her colleagues included "What do we throw away? Said another way, 'What are we spending time, money, and energy on that's not adding value anymore?" Cole often chased this question with, "When do we say no? And that question is about missed opportunities. When do we say no to employees? When do we say no to customers?"[4] The pattern of no's can be particularly helpful to examine if you find yourself in Responsible Stewardship. Has someone built a "house of no"—a term we started using when we were working to change a particularly creaky organization—inside your organization? Who are the organization's gatekeepers, and are they truly serving the interests of the business? What are the fears and anxieties underneath their resistance? Can you surface and address them directly?

Whatever your list of questions ends up looking like, consider first asking some of them in the form of a confidential survey, which invites people to reflect independently before engaging

---

*Argyris argued that leaders spend far too much time in advocacy, persuading others that their view of the world is correct, a phenomenon that gets worse as you move up the hierarchy.

with each other. A survey also uses writing—still our species' best tool for thinking—to deepen and reveal what's on every-body's minds. Pick someone relatively neutral to analyze the responses and report back to the group with summarized themes and observations. Strip out attribution to specific voices, even if those voices may be decipherable to the room. At this stage, peo-ple often discover that their colleagues have reached different conclusions from the same "facts" and/or are working with a dif-ferent set of facts entirely.

A survey can also help to account for differences in status in the room, the reality that some people may be walking in feeling valued and seen—high up on the Inclusion Dial*—while others may not be, for all kinds of reasons. Collecting perspectives in advance, confidentially, lowers the stakes of speaking up. Go fur-ther by making any process anxieties discussable: What could get in the way of our mandate? What concerns are each of us bring-ing to this conversation? These kinds of questions don't negate the disparities in participant status and stakes, but by naming them, you make it more possible to work around them.

Now tap a skilled facilitator to manage the conversation—the team member most likely to create a space where a range of peo-ple with different skills and experiences can engage productively with one another. As you get into conversation with one another, fight the impulse to converge early around one point of view. Celebrate the voices that are willing to offer a different take. Use prompts like "Who has a different perspective?" or, even better,

---

*This is our preferred metaphor for the progressive experience of inclusion in the workplace, ranging from feeling a base-level safety to feeling truly valued and cham-pioned. We'll explore this framework in detail on Wednesday.

"Who can *articulate* a different perspective?" By asking someone to describe a position they may or may not hold, you're making it easier to disagree with the group.

> **GUT CHECK:** Proceed when you have a short list of the organization's most significant problems.

Pick a Candidate Problem to Solve

Work with the team to pick a problem to solve *first*. One advantage of high-trust/high-speed leadership is that you get to reduce the anxiety of prioritization. In the new culture of problem-solving you're building, choosing not to focus on a problem right now doesn't mean *no*; it means *not now* (and *not now* means *not today* instead of *not this month*, which might as well mean never in some organizations). When you fix problems instead of tolerating them, everyone can begin to relax with the confidence that the organization is willing to take action. If this sequence seems highly unlikely in your company, see "Ten Signs Your Organization is Stalling."

For now, pick a place to begin. One way we like to get there is to summarize the problems that have surfaced in the discussion so far, in the form of relatively simple statements. Keep the industry jargon and functional shorthand to a minimum. Imagine you're explaining the problem to a family member who knows little about what you do all day.* For some of you, your list might look

---

*We like to imagine our mothers in the room, both fiercely intelligent women with an uncanny ability to sniff out phoniness. What are you hiding, they might ask, behind all those silly words?

something like this, with different parts of the business competing for attention:

1. We're not innovating fast enough.

2. Our customers can't tell us apart from our competitors anymore.

3. Our leaders aren't representative of the rest of our employees.

For those of you who started this process with a clear catalyst or presenting problem, try going a layer or two down in your analysis. For example, if good people are now leaving the company at high rates, what are some reasonable explanations for their exodus? Again, describe your theories in brief, accessible language:

1. Our people want more autonomy than we've been willing to give them.

2. Some employees aren't advancing in their careers at a fast enough rate.

3. Our culture tolerates and sometimes rewards assholery.*

Ask everyone to vote on the list, preferably without being influenced by one another, and see which problem emerges with the most heat around it. For the rest of the day, you'll be testing the

---

*This is a technical term made discussable in polite company thanks to the excellent scholarship of Bob Sutton, whose best-selling book, *The No Asshole Rule* (New York: Warner Business Books, 2007), changed the way the world viewed firm culture. Sutton documented the often-hidden organizational costs of rewarding high performers who overtly undermine company values or the basic norms of human decency.

team's thinking with additional data and input, so there's no need to hold on too tightly to a particular point of view. Trust your colleagues and simply document what's getting the most attention.

If the problem is clear to everyone at this point, move on with confidence that you have a theory of the case that's strong enough to test and refine. And if reasonable people can disagree—if more than one problem is vying for the top spot—pick one and make a commitment to one another that you're going to address the other ones soon, ideally with a specific time commitment (what's everyone doing *next* Monday?).

> **GUT CHECK:** Proceed when you've picked a candidate problem to solve and can describe it in simple, jargon-free language.

Collect the Organization's Problem Data

Now that you have a candidate problem, gather whatever data you have that might be relevant to the issue. We call this preexisting information *Sunday night data* (get it?), which simply means information the company *already* has before getting started on Monday activities. The idea here is to pause and make this data accessible—a nontrivial challenge in many organizations—and reduce the inevitable information disparities among problem hunters.

In effect, you're establishing a shareable set of facts, which has been generated by the measurement decisions you've historically made. And while your problem is likely to be lurking in

Ten Signs Your Organization Is Stalling

Not every organization is eager to solve its problems, a cultural barrier that may need to be resolved at some point on Monday. This is a pattern we see most frequently in companies in Responsible Stewardship. In the absence of an obvious performance crisis, leaders are clutching the status quo and underweighting its risks. This type of resistance to change can show up in many forms, some of them hard to decipher. Here are ten signs your company may be trying to slow you down, from wherever you're trying to lead in the hierarchy.*

1. **A task force is being assigned to the problem.** A small, intrepid team of reformers is one thing; indeed, it's the thing we're recommending to accelerate action today. Most task forces, it turns out, do not fit this profile. How can you tell? If you're being asked to rely on a structure or process that lacks status, legitimacy, or decision rights—or the sponsorship of someone who has any of the above— then it's unlikely to help you make a difference.

2. **You're being thanked for your time and effort.** If you suspect you're being indulged and dismissed, then you probably are. By the way, this is not the same thing as being disagreed with, which is a perfectly acceptable response to wherever your diagnostics lead you today. Your obligation as a changemaker is to make the persuasive case for your ideas. Your colleagues' obligation is to engage with them in good faith, not to uncritically agree with you.

3. **People doubt whether the organization (really) has a problem.** Be prepared for some of your colleagues to push back on your premise that the company has a
(continued)

problem. Hard truths are, by definition, difficult to face; this is particularly true for data that suggests cultural issues such as a lack of full inclusion. Stay strong. Be fluent in the evidence you gather today that the problem truly exists—and in resonant stories about the price the organization is paying for it.

4. **You're asked to respond to the grave concerns of unidentified critics.** These exchanges often start with some variation on, "As your friend, I think you should know what people are saying." This is usually a tactic to keep you in check rather than empower you with helpful information. Don't take the bait and react to rumor and hearsay. Encourage your critics to reveal themselves so that you can engage directly with their concerns, which may very well be valid. Collaboration happens in daylight.

5. **The specter of "legal issues" is being invoked.** The antidote to this one is to work directly with the legal team, which is often made up of people who are far more creative, flexible, and solutions-oriented than the detractors who are using their name. Lawyers are rarely the risk-intolerant killjoys they're made out to be by non-lawyers, so partner with them early.

6. **Your colleagues point out all the *other* problems that need to be solved.** This response assumes there's some kind of measurable limit on a firm's capacity to absorb positive change—and you're getting dangerously close to that line. People tend to underestimate their company's capacity to adapt to a better reality (as well as the true cost of continued inaction). The problem you surface today deserves a rapid response that reflects the

frustration, the mediocrity, and, in some organizations, the real pain of the status quo.

7. **You keep hearing about a future state where the conditions for change will be much, much better.** This may be the most common expression of resistance we see: the fantasy that it's going to be easier to change things at some point in the future. In our experience, this is almost never the case, and the opposite is usually true. The clarity and momentum you have right now are tremendous assets, but they're also perishable ones. In most cases, the "fierce urgency of now" wins the day, particularly when the success and well-being of the people around you are on the line.

8. **The timeline for action is growing.** This is another common delay tactic, a proposed antidote to the concerns expressed in items 6 and 7. Your diagnosis is embraced at a conceptual level, but the proposed timetable for change is long and vague. Treat this development as an existential threat not just to Monday, but to the whole week. When it comes to solving mission-critical problems, the right time to take action is now.

9. **Your colleagues think they can wait you out.** Management thought leader Earl Sasser calls this "kidney stone management"—the assumption that this, too, shall pass. Make it clear that you're not going anywhere, preferably with a smile. If you're not the boss, then show up in her office with a cup of coffee, just the way she likes it, every morning until you get her to engage. That move, by the way, has never failed us.

(continued)

10. You keep hearing, "We've already tried that." The company may have already wrestled with some version of the problem you've surfaced, with little to show for it beyond a legacy of frustration and cynicism. If so, do your homework and learn what you can from whatever went wrong. Regardless, context changes, including the very material context of your willingness to lead on these issues. *You* haven't tried before, which is going to make all the difference.

*This is an updated version of a fan-favorite list we originally shared in *Unleashed* (Boston: Harvard Business Review Press, 2020).

places you *haven't* measured, the indirect price you're paying for the problem will still be showing up somewhere in the data. One outcome of the week ahead will be to start to see these kinds of connections more clearly.

What's fair game? In short, whatever might help you to better understand your problem, erring on the side of more. The pile will look different based on your own context, but here's a working list of potentially useful inputs to spark your own thinking:

- Mission/vision/values statements

- Recent investor decks, board decks, analyst reports

- Strategy documents (e.g., business plans, product road maps)

- Multiyear financial statements

- Customer acquisition/churn/segmentation data

- Customer surveys and feedback data

- Employee sentiment data (e.g., engagement surveys, exit interviews)

- Employee achievement data (e.g., promotion and retention data)

- Hot-spot information (e.g., press articles, town hall transcripts, company message boards)

Essentially, *any* existing data you have is in play here. When Christine Keung, former chief data officer for the City of San Jose, was trying to figure out how to improve programming for the city's low-income families, she and her team dug into ten years of administrative records on scholarship registrations. They learned that more than 95 percent of program scholarship recipients lived 1.5 miles or less from the nearest community center. As they analyzed the data and consulted actively with their frontline teams, they began to understand why. Scholarships were advertised only on posters and flyers at community centers, which meant that the city was unintentionally privileging residents who happened to live nearby.

To solve the problem, Keung's team focused on driving awareness throughout San Jose, increasing the city's presence on social media and through creative, low-cost advertising. When Keung reflected on the project's success, she highlighted the value of changing the organization's relationship with information: "Our impact was about empowering city staff with insight and options that data can achieve, informing not only big, strategic decisions, but also improving the thousands of small decisions that impact resident experience. . . . a local government that can't capture local context misses the point."[5]

Keung and her team made quick progress by opening up access to their problem data and pushing it all the way to the front lines. For some organizations, this type of empowerment will require overcoming the impulse to be protective of information, even with your fellow Monday travelers. Many companies, particularly more mature ones, end up hiding the data that's needed to effectively solve problems behind a culture of restricted access. That doesn't mean *everyone* in the company, much less the broader public, gets access to this information. In fact, broadcasting information early in the process, without having a plan for what to do about it, can slow down and even sabotage the change mission.

When we worked with a large company to help accelerate its DEI work, the pressure to share data widely was high right from the start, even before the company fully understood the problem it was trying to solve (much less had a confidence-inspiring plan to solve it). We did share the numbers eventually, but only after the company put a strong DEI strategy and leadership team in place. The material word here is *eventually*. On Thursday—also known as *storytelling day*—you're likely to invoke some of this data as you make a powerful case for change to your colleagues. For now, your job is to get clear on the facts and share them with the people who are helping you.

> **GUT CHECK:** Proceed when you've gathered the data that's relevant to your problem and shared it with your fellow problem hunters.

Build a Case with the Data You Have

What can you learn from your Sunday night data? The rest of this chapter is about talking with stakeholders and gathering new data, but before you get anyone else involved, let's see how far you can get with the information you already have. This is the step where you may want to put your data analyst to work.

When AJ Hubbard, former global executive of inclusion and diversity at GE Appliances (GEA), began working on culture change at the company, he pushed GEA to first understand its starting place. "I was told this was an organization of operators," he recalled, "[with an ethos of] 'Tell me what to do and where to go'. . . . I flipped that on its head. . . . I can give you recommendations, but I would rather us together look at the data . . . who's joining the company, who's leaving, who's getting promoted, who's considered high-potential."[6] Hubbard and his operations team eventually created a dashboard that made it easy to access, analyze, and make use of the data the company was already collecting. As a first step, Hubbard insisted on learning from what GEA already knew or *should* have known.

One way to build cynicism quickly in an organization—something we see all the time, by the way—is to ask people for their input and then do very little with the information they give you (and take a long time to do even that). This is particularly common in the annual culture survey ritual. Many companies collect data about their employees' disengagement and frustration, and then do nothing visible to address these problems except ask about it again the following year. As you move through the activities of this week, reflect on our favorite prompt: What would change if you treated *other people's* time as your company's most strategic asset? Who would you become as a colleague and leader? Who might those other people become when they're around you?

Use this data to try to prove to yourselves that your theory of the case is right. If you're tackling a strategy issue, for example, pick a framework for analysis that allows you to think about the problem in a more systematic way.[7] If it's a culture problem, go back to those exit interviews and companywide surveys. If it's a capability or operations problem, look for patterns in customer complaints. Document the gaps between what your sales team is selling and what the company is reliably delivering. How would you know, right now, that the thing you want to fix is really broken?

The varsity version of this is to do additional analysis on your existing data, using the lens of your problem statement to guide your process. In other words, send your analyst into the data with a more specific set of questions. If you're wrestling with high employee frustration, for example, then what patterns can they find in who isn't thriving? Is it everyone or specific groups? If it's specific groups, then which career stages are generating the most heat? Which functions? Which demographic profiles?

Additional analysis like this can be particularly helpful for problems that feel overwhelming at first, issues that may be charged with emotion or complicated by factors outside the organization's control. A feature of a move-fast-and-fix-things mindset is that being overwhelmed or confused or afraid does not give you license to stand still. Instead, these are signals to get moving before frustration tips into organizational anxiety or even despair. You can't control every variable, but you can get in touch with the agency you *do* have, which is likely to be greater than you think. Grounding the case for your problem in data can be one important step in that direction.

For any company wrestling with DEI challenges, we've found that clear, rigorous analysis of the problem can be particularly helpful. You may not be able to solve the larger societal context of injustice and division, but you can rebuild trust on your own team and root out the inequities in your own organization. As we've written about before, when we spent some time with WeWork to help build a stronger culture of gender equity, we took a closer look at its existing data to better understand the experience of female candidates at various points in its hiring pipeline. In addition to the demographics of who was being hired, we looked at who was being screened out, who was brought in for an interview, who made it to the final stages, and so on. In a healthy recruiting process, demographic proportions should remain fairly consistent from one stage to another. If 40 percent of people in your screening stages are women, then roughly 40 percent should be getting to the interview stage. If those numbers shift significantly from stage to stage, then the process likely needs some attention.

This type of analysis can lead you to very actionable solutions. For example, in another company we advised, shifting demographics in the hiring pipeline were explained by a hiring manager who was less familiar with the gaps in experience that working moms often had. The granularity of this kind of analysis often gives you enough information to make fast progress, which in this case was a brief, low-stakes conversation with a single employee.

This kind of detailed analysis at this stage in the process may not be useful to every problem in every company. If you're rewarding assholery, for example, you might just want to confirm the patterns of engagement and departure around the company's worst offenders (everyone knows who they are). Are promising junior associates avoiding a particular senior partner? Are people more likely to leave after working with them? Whatever the nature of the problem, the point of these activities is to follow AJ Hubbard's lead and figure out what you already know before uncovering what you *don't*.

> **GUT CHECK:** Proceed when you've learned
> as much as you can about your problem
> from the data you already have.

Learn More about Your Problem

We advise most companies to start their pursuit of *new* data by learning from the stakeholders most impacted by a problem. For example, if your analytics revealed that military veterans are struggling to get promoted or that Black women are leaving the company at disproportionately high rates, then you now know who to talk to next about the problem. Resist the instinct to make it much more complicated than this.

Your main tactic here will be conversation. You can dress up these interactions in the formal wear of interviews and focus groups, which can help to signal that the company takes the problem seriously. But you can also be more informal and opportunistic: a cup of coffee with a colleague, questions tacked onto the end of a standing meeting, a sales call with your best customer that you gracefully extend. We call this less formal approach *lounge-wear conversation,* and for some problems, in some settings, it's going to get you better information.

Try blending the two approaches. We'll often do structured focus groups and then ask a few participants for an informal follow-up call. Sometimes these are the most active or insightful participants in the discussion, but we also follow up with those who were reluctant to engage. We've sometimes gained the most insight into a problem by learning from the people most hesitant to talk about it.

Your job in these conversations is to listen—*really* listen—with the curiosity of an anthropologist and the accountability of a leader. Draft a set of questions in advance, informed by the work you've already done today, that will signal that you respect your audience and have put some real advance thought into the issue. Document what you hear on the surface in these discussions, but also observe the nonverbal communication in the room. How are people responding to the discussion? To you? To each other?

When our colleague Hubert Joly led the turnaround of tech retailer Best Buy, one of his first decisions was to huddle personally with his frontline team to better understand the commercially devastating practice of showrooming. Customers had developed a very rational habit of visiting Best Buy stores, getting a personalized product education courtesy of well-trained employees, and then going home to buy from cheaper, more convenient suppliers such as Amazon. Under Joly's leadership, Best Buy quickly announced it would match online prices and launched its innovative Store Pickup system (online purchases would be ready for pickup in real life within an hour), undermining its competitors' biggest advantages at a speed that would have been unheard of pre-Joly. The seeds of these ideas were planted in Joly's dialogue with employees in the earliest days of his tenure.[8]

Keep in mind—always—that it will be riskier for some people to share their honest perspectives. Make it easier by ensuring confidentiality. If you end up wanting to use someone's name in a future discussion, circle back and get their permission to do so. This is also an opportunity to be intentional about who you're sending into which communities to have which types of conversations. Recruit facilitators from your diagnostics team, but don't hesitate to deputize others if it makes sense for the problem you're trying to fix.

Let's say your problem is strategy—the market can no longer distinguish you from your competitors—and so it's customers you've decided to engage at this point. This might be a great use of your best salesperson, for example, or even your CEO. What do your customers care most about? What do they care less about? Would they be willing to pay a premium for something your company can uniquely deliver? This is the type of conversation you've earned the right to have after moving through the previous Monday activities. Now send in the right person to have it.

Intuit founder Scott Cook would urge you to *observe* customer behavior, as well. Cook developed the company's legendary "follow me home" program, which sends Intuit employees home with consenting customers to observe them using the company's products. Cook attributes much of the company's success to the practice and the ethos that drives it: openness, humility, attentiveness.[9] The program emphasizes observation over customer commentary and deploys multiple employees per home visit because different employees will observe different things (more on the power of difference later in the week). Intuit conducts more than ten thousand hours of these visits a year, and the CEO has been known to clock up to one hundred of those hours. "What you get from a [home visit] you can't get from a data stream," former CEO Brad Smith reflected. "You've got to look somebody in the eye and feel the emotion."[10]

For any team working on why a specific group of people in the organization isn't thriving, we suggest pairing a discussion about "big" issues (for example, barriers to advancement) with a discussion about the so-called smaller ones. These are things that may seem trivial on the surface, things your best employees are often reluctant to complain about for fear of looking like they're not team players. But they are also the things that can have outsize signaling value and point you in the direction of larger issues.

We call this discussion *the indignities list*, since it's meant to surface the nicks and bruises of daily life at your company, the stressors that chip away at the full dignity of your colleagues. Indignities are often born of blind spots and representation gaps, which is why they're almost never equitably distributed.* They're also usually highly fixable with minimal effort and investment.

When one hospital system was dealing with high churn on its nursing team at the height of the Covid-19 pandemic, it had a

---

*If the life experience of decision-makers differs materially from the bulk of your employees, we guarantee that the dignity of your employees is being undercut somewhere.

series of very direct conversations with the nurses themselves. There were big problems that the company needed to solve—issues with compensation and job design—but there were also smaller ones that contributed to the exodus of mission-critical talent. One indignity that surfaced in these discussions was a pattern where relatively cheap, poorly serviced copier machines would break easily and not be fixed with any sense of urgency. A broken copier machine meant that a nurse already burdened by a high administrative load had to go from floor to floor looking for a working machine. Those extra steps weren't a big deal on any given day, but the fact that the company was making nurses' jobs even harder reinforced the impression that nurses were under-seen and undervalued.[11]

Imagine how far an urgent investment in good copiers and a proactive maintenance plan would have gone in this situation. To be clear, that distance is not just about fixing the copiers; it's also about the process that would have led to that investment, the new lines of communication that would have been opened to surface the problem, the engagement with the larger issues that the broken copiers signified. That's the spirit of Monday—of the entire week, really—to help you pivot from reactive firefighting to confident, proactive fire *prevention*.*

> **GUT CHECK:** Proceed when you've gained new perspective on your problem from the stakeholders most impacted by it.

*Remember Smokey the Bear? Only *you*, it turns out, can prevent organizational fires.

Decide What You're Going to Fix This Week

Regroup with your problem hunters—both the original team and anyone you deputized along the way—and debrief what you've learned today. Was your theory of the case correct? Which root causes had true explanatory power? What surprised and inspired and unsettled everyone along the way?

After Hubert Joly completed his own version of Monday at Best Buy, he identified the root cause of the problems he was seeing as a fundamentally transactional culture. Instead of hawking TVs and computers that were easily substitutable, Joly resolved to inject a higher purpose into the company and rebuild its strategy, operations, and economics to deliver on a new promise: enrich the lives of its customers through technology. That clarity was only possible because he first committed to *solve the right problem*. What at first glance looked like a relatively simple consumer behavior issue—showrooming—turned out to be something much deeper.

Like Joly, you may uncover a root cause that surprises you or you may have been right about your problem all along. All we can tell you, from our experience, is that it's almost impossible to know at the start of the week which camp you're going to be in—and that it's certainly worth spending a "day" finding out.

As you close out your Monday effort, the goal of this final huddle is to gain buy-in on the problem the company will solve *next*. Choose one with elevated urgency, one that's the clearest source of disruption and distraction. Describe what you're going to fix with the richness and specificity you just earned. For example, instead of "Our strategy isn't working," think "Our play-it-safe strategy is designed to not disappoint anyone rather than truly delight our best customers." Make the case to each other in language that inspires action. What are the stakes of this urgent, solvable problem? Why is it worth everyone's time to move fast and fix it?

A final note before we wrap for today: congratulations. Monday is a do-it-yourself adventure that looks different for every organization. But what's universal is that if you take these steps, then you'll identify at least one meaningful barrier to Accelerating Excellence. And if you do it our way, relying on your own team and moving faster than seemed prudent or even possible, then it will cost you almost nothing for an immeasurable payoff.

> **GUT CHECK:** Proceed when you've identified the right problem to solve.

TUESDAY

Solve for Trust

ood morning! That new feeling you're feeling today is what we call *Tuesday morning confidence*. It's the confidence that comes from solving the right problems and, more generally, distinguishing between activity and impact—between doing things and doing things that will make a difference to your organization.

Tuesday morning confidence is the absence of pretense and swagger, which are powerful temptations on the leadership path (ones we haven't always been able to resist ourselves). In fact, one way to think about what you're doing this week is that you're no longer *pretending*. On Monday you stopped pretending that you knew which problem to solve without first challenging your thinking and gathering more data. Today you'll stop pretending that you know *how* to solve the problem without first testing your ideas and finding out if they work.

Your mission for today is to create a *Good Enough Plan.** A Good Enough Plan is a plan to build and rebuild trust with the stakeholders at the center of your problem. We sometimes refer to Tuesday as your *sandbox day* because we want you to get into the organizational sandbox and play. We want you to be in motion today, creating the conditions to learn, far outside the walls of what David Foster Wallace famously called "our own tiny skull-sized kingdoms."[1] We want you to try new things today and pay attention to whatever happens next. We want you to bring some lightness—even some joy—to this process, even when the stakes are high, which is when you're going to need that joy the most.

Our motto for this phase of the work is "Find new beeps" (hang in there with us). One of Frances's favorite sessions with MBA students is a team-based exercise called the Electric Maze. Teams must find the one true path through a floor maze of identical squares, and they get only two types of feedback along the way: a loud, aggressive beep when a teammate steps on the "wrong" square, and a satisfying silence when they step on the "right" one. Oh, and for good measure, no talking is allowed. Teams can communicate only through writing or hand gestures, which simulates the communication challenges of the modern organization.[2]

Without ruining future opportunities for experiential learning, we'll just say that the teams that do best are the ones that are fast, intentional, and downright cheerful in their pursuit of

---

*A Good Enough Plan is distinct from *the perfect plan,* which is an elusive, fantastical creature that has never actually been spotted in the wild. Searching for the perfect plan has slowed down many a sentimental operator with dreams of perfectionist glory.

TUESDAY'S AGENDA

1. Fail with enthusiasm.

2. Find your organization's "trust wobble."

3. Do a business model checkup.

4. Make your people better.

5. Change how you work.

6. Identify "new" talent.

7. Make the difficult people decisions.

8. Don't make it all about you.

9. Walk the talk.

Materials You'll Need for Today

- Optimism

- Refusal to be paralyzed by complexity

- Commitment to embrace *intelligent failure* (aka new beeps), defined simply as unsuccessful trials[3]

- Willingness to advance some people, separate from others

- Direct operating knowledge or good access to operators who know how things work

- A wide selection of adult beverages*

*By *adult beverage* we mean celebratory and dignified, liquid punctuation for a good day's work. Alcohol is an optional active ingredient. Frances's favorite adult beverage, for example, is fancy tonic water, chilled and neat.

new beeps. They treat every new beep as an exhilarating development that brings them closer to a solution. That's how we want you to feel all day Tuesday, which means that curious inner scientist of yours may want to stick around for another day—the one who knows exactly what to do with unsolved problems: run smart experiments.

Fail with Enthusiasm

At NerdWallet, a personal finance company with impressive growth and a standout consumer brand, failure is treated as the foundation for success. This idea is reinforced by a prominent office "Fail Wall," where employees leave sticky-note records of their mistakes. For example, CEO Tim Chen used the Fail Wall to reflect on his missteps in hiring a public relations firm: "I tried to outsource PR to an agency, idea generation and all. We got five press hits in six months." The Fail Wall is covered with stickies.[4]

How would a Fail Wall play in your organization? On your team? In your own tiny skull-sized kingdom? Chen's cofounder, Jake Gibson, explained the logic of the wall this way: "Employees must think of every action as an experiment rather than as something on which they'll be graded 'pass' or 'fail.'"[5] This can be a mindset shift for many of us, who have been trained on a long game of avoiding mistakes, a game with very simple rules: success is good, failure is bad, full stop. But intelligent failure, the kind of failure that teaches you something important, is near the top of the list of your team's most valuable assets. As the Electric

Maze teaches us, the fastest path to what works is to learn systematically from what *doesn't*.

When Google, famous for its relentless experimentation engine, tried to estimate its own intelligent failure number, it found that 80 to 90 percent of its controlled experiments fail in the sense that they generate negative results.[6] Said differently, Google's elite technical leaders make incorrect predictions (aka mistakes) *more than 80 percent of the time*. And yet we often treat our own mistakes as unwelcome, unexpected bogeymen, revealing that we somehow expect our personal failure rate to be hovering near zero. The only way to get close to that number is by not even trying to solve problems. To stick with our maze metaphor, you would have to refuse to even step on the first square. Those of you stuck in Responsible Stewardship may be experiencing some version of this at the scale of your organization.

We suggest being Fail Wall–direct with your team—and yourself—that the objective of this stage is not *to be right*; the objective of this stage is *to learn*. We use the word *pilot* as frequently as we can in our work because it reinforces this message. The concept of a pilot project has been around for a long time, and yet it's still being underutilized as a *mindset*. You can think of your Good Enough Plan as a collection of pilot projects designed to solve your problem. Is your plan going to work? Probably not, at least not the first iteration of it. Is it going to get you closer to figuring out what *will*? Absolutely.

> **GUT CHECK:** Proceed when you're willing to embrace failure as an essential source of learning.

Find Your Organization's "Trust Wobble"

Where should you begin to experiment? The short answer is to try anything you think has a reasonable chance of working and then—here's the catch—*don't be attached to the results*. Whether the ideas you're piloting succeed or fail is information, so work to produce as much of it as possible. The point, again, is to learn.

Should you fix systems or people? Hire innovators or create a culture of innovation? Better train your people or redesign the way they work? The answer is yes. Do all of it, with ambition and urgency, which you are earning the right to have this week. We will lay out your options in a logical order because that's how books work, but don't overthink the sequencing. Instead, chase the steepest, fastest learning curve the organization will tolerate (which is often steeper and faster than you think it will be). You'll be in racing shape by Friday, but today is a chance to rev the organization's engine.

As you start to brainstorm pilot solutions, we suggest looking at your problem from the perspective of the stakeholder at the center of it. Are *shareholders* disappointed in the company's profitability? Are *customers* jumping ship for your competitors? Are Gen Z *employees* frustrated and leaving at an accelerated rate? Make the issue personal, literally, by identifying the person(s) with the highest stake in your problem. You hopefully learned a lot about the perspective of those persons in the discussions you had yesterday.*

---

*If that's not the case and an unexpected protagonist emerges at this point, pause and do another round of Monday-ish data gathering.

If you're thinking about your problem in stakeholder-free terms, then add a stakeholder to the story. If your problem is a high burn rate, for example, reflect on who's paying the biggest price for it. Is it your investors whose money you're spending (and who may be on the hook for the next financing round)? Or is it your colleagues who are starting to question the company's viability? Pick one, for now, and really try to feel their pain. (If you can't feel it for whatever reason, then you're not done gathering data.)

One way to frame your problem is that the organization has lost trust with this stakeholder. Just like personal trust, we've found that organizational trust relies on the presence of authenticity, empathy, and logic (see figure 2-1).[7]

FIGURE 2-1

Key drivers of organizational trust

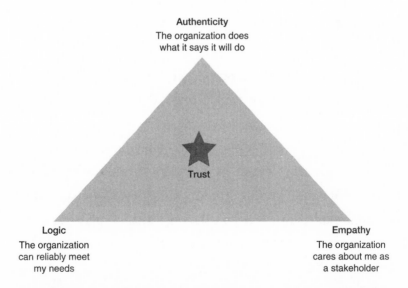

Authenticity
The organization does
what it says it will do

Trust

Logic
The organization
can reliably meet
my needs

Empathy
The organization
cares about me as
a stakeholder

Source: Adapted from Frances Frei and Anne Morriss, *Unleashed: The Unapologetic Leader's Guide to Empowering Everyone Around You* (Boston: Harvard Business Review Press, 2020).

In order to trust you as an *organization*, your stakeholders need to believe that you care about them (empathy), that you're capable of meeting their needs (logic), and that you can be expected to do what you say you'll do (authenticity). Just like when *people* lose trust, organizations that are losing trust—or failing to build as much trust as they could—tend to get shaky or *wobble* on one of these three dimensions.

Revisit the problem you surfaced on Monday through this lens. Does the stakeholder at the center of your problem question your company's empathy, logic, or authenticity? If your customers are losing trust, for example, are they questioning your price hike with so many new competitors in the market (logic)? Or do they feel like they can't get anyone on the phone when they have a problem (empathy)? Or is your CEO making commitments that your sales team can't deliver on (authenticity)?

What's *your* company's primary wobble? And what are your best ideas for how to steady it? See "Ten Organizational Trust Pitfalls" for some initial inspiration. Throughout the rest of the day, we're going to explore some investments in logic, empathy, and authenticity that we know work at the scale of an organization. These are levers you can pull that can have big, fast impact on your organization. We're going to spend more time on people experiments than product experiments because while product experiments are common (thank you, Google), we see far less experimentation in the rest of the business—and, in particular, in setting your very human resources up for success. It's also true, in our experience, that most of your problems are likely to be showing up in human form. While your own Good Enough Plan will be highly customized to your own conditions, we

Ten Organizational Trust Pitfalls

Tolstoy famously started *Anna Karenina* by asserting that all happy families are alike, while unhappy families are uniquely unhappy. Organizations tend to be more predictable despite how *familial* the dysfunction sometimes feels. While the context of every firm is novel, its problems tend to be more commonplace. Below is a list of some of the trust problems we see most frequently in our work, along with what they reveal about what's getting wobbly.

1. **Aversion to making choices.** This one can present in all kinds of ways, from managing for consensus to trying to be great at everything you do as an organization. A gentle reminder: although it may feel safer to hedge your bets, catering to a constituent that can be best described as "everyone" is often a much riskier path for the company. Your refusal to choose is increasing the likelihood of exhausted mediocrity. *Trust wobble: logic.*

2. **Reliance on heroic employees.** Many business models are designed for employees we wish we had, not for the employees we actually have—the ones with imperfections and lives outside of work. If your operations depend on people continuously going above and beyond, then be prepared to work much harder to find these magical creatures and reward them with outsize compensation. Few organizations are truly up for the task. *Trust wobble: logic.*

3. **Shiny object syndrome.** The human brain is wired to focus on the new, new thing, even when the old, old thing matters more. A lack of intention (also known, less cheerily, as lack of *discipline*) in the pursuit of new opportunities

(continued)

puts your business model at risk. Excellent adventures in new products and markets are often justified by hazy ROI equations that inflate the upside and downplay the risk, including the cost of distraction from more urgent priorities. May be accompanied by other types of magical thinking. *Trust wobble: logic.*

4. **Disengaged middle management.** Managers in what we call the "murky middle" of an organization are often the only people who know the true distance between a company's reality and its ambition. They know how much effort it's going to take to win, understand the true hazards of the journey, and typically have the most to lose (and least to gain) along the way. And yet. Instead of being unleashed in moments of big change, middle managers are often overlooked by a leadership team that's focused on inspiring the front lines and gaining buy-in at the top. *Trust wobble: empathy.*

5. **Casual relationship with other people's time.** Do you treat your people's time as if it's your most strategic asset? It's one of our favorite leadership reflection prompts, and you'll hear us repeat it again and again. Far too many organizations are far too comfortable wasting their employees' time on everything from clunky HR technology to forcing everyone to come into the office to indulge a nostalgic view of what work used to feel like. The opportunity cost is immeasurable. *Trust wobble: empathy.*

6. **Comfort with collateral damage.** This is the "break things" part of "Move fast and break things," which can get embedded into an organization's culture. It often presents as desensitization to unintentional harms and justified by a "We tried our best" storyline. Organizations that would

never tolerate this attitude when it comes to some parts of the business ("We tried our best to protect our financial data!") often want participation trophies for *trying* not to harm their users and employees. *Trust wobble: empathy.*

7. **High incidence of the "Sunday scaries."** If a significant percentage of your colleagues feel an impending sense of dread at the thought of coming to work, then something is strained, if not broken, in the company's relationship with its employees. Sometimes there's an unskilled (or worse) manager to blame, but when people are experiencing this kind of anticipatory anxiety at scale, then there's an org-level problem that needs to be fixed. Skip ahead to Wednesday, which will help you get in touch with the true price of fear. (*Spoiler:* You're getting a small fraction of what your people are capable of contributing.) *Trust wobble: empathy.*

8. **People-pleasing in the boardroom.** This pattern essentially comes down to our human impulse to tell people what we think they want to hear, particularly when said people can materially impact our organizational and/or professional futures. We're not talking about fraud or misrepresentation here but rather a habit of gently withholding, massaging, and constructing reality. The trust hit for this one is often higher than we think, since our audience tends to be sensitive to being managed and is composed of excellent detectors of partial truths. Know that what they really want from you is information that allows them to help the company solve problems. *Trust wobble: authenticity.*

9. **Tolerance for misalignment.** Is your marketing team writing checks that your product team can't cash?* Lack of

(*continued*)

alignment anywhere in the business is a problem, but pay closest attention to org-level disconnects. One we see frequently is a gap between strategy and culture—for example, a strategy of innovation layered onto a culture defined by coloring within the lines. *Trust wobble: authenticity.*

10. **Delusions of meritocracy.** OK, here's what this looks like: you've told yourselves you're a meritocracy, but you keep hiring, promoting, and retaining the same types of people. If the humans at the top of your organization bear little resemblance to the rest of your employees, the customers you serve, or the demographic distribution of the communities in which you operate, then we promise you, you're not a meritocracy. *Trust wobble: authenticity.*

*For our younger readers: a *check* was a special piece of paper that you could turn into any denomination of currency you wanted by writing things on little designated lines.

hope you'll find some ideas in the pages ahead to at least get you started.

Depending on the nature of your problem, you'll also find a world of great insights and frameworks beyond this book to help you solve it. We encourage you to do your homework and make use of these resources, but what we care even more about is that you're taking action and trying new things *today.* Start with the trust-building ideas you and your colleagues already have, the ones that occur to you right now, before reading another page of this book or any other. Begin exploring your proverbial maze with the liberating truth of your situation: you have no idea what the path through is going to be.

GUT CHECK: Proceed when you have a working theory on the trust wobble at the center of your problem.

Do a Business Model Checkup

Some of you have surfaced a problem in your current strategy, value proposition, product-market fit, or funding mechanism. For simplicity, we're going to call this category your "business model." You're not meeting stakeholder needs because some part of your business model's *logic* is wobbly. For example, trust is breaking down in the airline industry right now because the basic logic of the sector's current value proposition—high ticket prices in exchange for unreliable service—doesn't make sense to us as consumers.

Spend the rest of the "day" (this may take you some time) working on your Good Enough Plan to fix it—and then test and improve that plan with rigor and optimism. Your mantra for this work is to "maximize new beeps, minimize time." In fact, our suggestion is to lovingly put down this book, at least for now, and go do that work. Come back when you've regained full confidence in the viability of your business model, which means you now have the luxury of solving other kinds of problems.

If you already have that confidence, we'd still encourage you to pause and kick the tires. While Uber's primary trust challenge was to steady the empathy wobbles in its relationship with a range of stakeholders (employees, drivers, regulators), the company also needed to convince shareholders of the *logic* of its long-term business plan, particularly its path to profitability.[8] Although some of these questions were reasonable to ask any company at Uber's stage, the company needed to start answering them. When that became clear, Uber immediately began executing a logic-driven strategy of focusing on the markets that were most defensible.[9]

That's the approach we suggest. Although your *primary* wobble(s) may be elsewhere, make sure there aren't any logic cracks in the foundation of your business model. When one team invited us in to help them rebuild trust with a key employee segment, we discovered that their trust challenge was more complex. The company was indeed losing trust with certain groups of employees, but there were also flaws in its business strategy, which hadn't been updated in decades. Sales were lumpy, and shareholders were getting restless. Instead of sequencing these challenges—show more *empathy* to employees and then more *logic* to shareholders—the company's challenge was to do both at the same time, which it did, with ambition and urgency.

Which brings us to the *interaction* of wobbles. Shareholder wobbles such as business model challenges can be powerfully distracting—particularly in young companies—and make it harder to focus on employee needs.* Conversely, comfort with collateral product damage can undermine the logic of your strategy when, for example, your users refuse to keep tolerating it. You don't need to untangle all these relationships, just be aware that they likely exist (and don't stop being curious once you've found your first wobble).

---

*One tell for this one is a lack of investment in a real HR skill set even when the company is teeming with employees.

Make Your People Better

A common source of wobbly organizational logic is when a workforce doesn't have all the skills to meet a particular stakeholder's needs. Said differently, there's some kind of *capability* gap between the work that has to be done and the team you've assembled to do that work.* Although this gap is more common in high-growth companies, where the needs of the organization are changing rapidly, we're seeing it everywhere now as the complexity of running *any* business spikes. We now tell leaders to just assume there's a capability gap somewhere in their operations. Your challenge is to find it before your customers feel it and your competitors exploit it.

Once you uncover a capability gap, you have three options for running experiments in how to close it: (1) upskill your people, (2) change the way they work, or (3) find "new" talent (not everyone may be so new). We suggest starting with the first one—also known as *development*—even though it's often not the place where many organizations like to start. If the pattern holds, development is going to take you further than you expect and generate all kinds of delightful benefits along the way, including higher loyalty, engagement, and job satisfaction from your colleagues who get to learn and grow at a faster rate. Say it with us: *My best people want to get better every day.*

*In our work we frequently use a framework that our colleague Ryan Buell developed, which pushes leaders to consider gaps in *motivation* and *license*, in addition to *capability*. For example, while a team may be capable, it may lack other important performance drivers such as a strong reward system (motivation) or clear decision rights (license). We suggest you start by addressing capability gaps, since they're the most common.

People are the only investment with the possibility of infinite returns, and yet we often stop behaving as if that's true once we onboard them. In a recent survey of 2,600 *Fortune* 1000 executives, more than 75 percent reported that development was inadequate at their companies.[10] Even in sophisticated organizations like these, even as the opportunities and challenges of the business continue to grow, we irrationally permit the learning curve of our teams to flatten out. This approach never made much sense, but it's now certainly nonsensical in this era of roiling markets, hurtling technology, and spiking uncertainty. The only chance we have of keeping up with the rate of change is to adapt and evolve more quickly. In the world of work, that means continuous development of our own skills and the skills of the people around us.

Airbnb's ambitious Data University was built on this conviction. The company thinks about data as "the voice of users at scale," which is framing we love. When it wanted to hear that voice in every function of the business, Airbnb first had to solve a logic problem: only a small, highly technical team knew how to work with data proficiently. In a blog post that reads more like a manifesto ("How Airbnb Democratizes Data Science"), the company explained that while "it wouldn't be possible to have a data scientist in every room—we [still] needed to scale our skill set."[11] Instead of trying to hire its way to increased capability, Airbnb rolled out a demanding, thirty-module curriculum that trained nontechnical employees in how to access, interpret, and integrate data into everyday decision-making. Within months of launching the program, thousands of weekly active users were accessing the company's central data platform, almost 50 percent of its payroll.[12]

Think of it this way: just as the annual performance review is now obsolete, replaced with more frequent and less formal performance discussions, so now is the annual development plan. We suggest at least a quarterly conversation with your direct reports about how they're going to upgrade their skills. What are they going to do *today* to get better? What about *tomorrow*? For some of you, the highlight of creating your Good Enough Plan will be asking your colleagues these questions for the first time.

The good news is that the answers can be cheaper and faster than ever before. Like Airbnb, if your challenge is to scale a capability or transfer skills from one part of the business to another, you may be able to solve the problem with internal resources. A gap in management skills, for example, may be closeable with strong mentoring or peer coaching programs that enable leaders to learn from one another. And if you can't get there internally, a wide range of external training resources are now low-cost or even free, thanks to digital distribution and remote learning.*

Keep in mind that development can be *formal* (e.g., structured training, executive coaching) or *informal* (e.g., access to stretch assignments). Formal development tends to be more efficient, particularly in environments that are growing or changing quickly. Exposure and experience are incredible teachers, but they often don't scale quickly enough when you need to upskill large numbers of people. One of the lessons of working with companies in hypergrowth is that when organizations are moving fast, there's rarely enough time and space for sufficient informal training and support, particularly for managers.

Pro tip: Our colleague Deepak Malhotra is one of the best negotiation minds on the planet, and he offers his advice *for free* in a series of must-watch YouTube videos.

A feature of our work in these environments has been management education to support employees who have been promoted into leadership roles they don't yet know how to do with excellence. Organizations that are growing quickly often cross their fingers and hope managers pick up all the skills they need before inflicting too much pain on their direct reports. Whenever executives assert to us that they have no other choice, the business is simply moving too fast, we often ask, "How's that working out for you?" Don't wait for someone else to ask you that question. Ask yourself how well your development strategy is working or, better yet, ask your employees. The answer may be downright *illogical*.

> **GUT CHECK:** Proceed when you're ready
> to invest shamelessly—and continuously—
> in the development of your people.

Change How You Work

For some of you, the fastest path to upping your organization's logic game is to change the way work happens. This is the category of experiments that reimagines roles, responsibilities, workflows, reporting lines, organizational structure, and/or decision rights. At the individual level, this could mean a change in someone's job design so that they have more bandwidth or more license to solve problems effectively. At the team or functional level, it could mean integrating AI into your operating plan or leaning into agile development practices. At the company level, it could mean launching new divisions, things like shared back-end services or experimenting with a four-day workweek. Think of it as a change in the *how* rather than the *who* or the *what*.

Changing how you work could also mean changing how you partner with resources outside the formal boundaries of the organization—other people and organizations who can help you meet your stakeholders' needs more effectively. This is what Apple did when it opened up its App Store to outside developers, a bold bet on logic that made customers better off but wasn't so easy for the famously insular company.[13]

When Frances had the pleasure of speaking with Apple's senior team in the early 2000s, a few years before the App Store launched, a gatekeeper in the process asked her to send her slides in advance of the session to ensure they would meet the company's famously high design standards. Our most loyal readers will not be surprised to learn that said gatekeeper was appalled at the state of Frances's slides, which were aggressively uninspired (too much, honey?), limited by whatever PowerPoint art had been available in the previous decade.* Frances was told, literally, "You can't show those slides here." She was delighted by the exchange, which created a fantastic opening story for the new focus of her talk: the strategic risks of walled-off organizations.

Our point is simply to be open to experimenting with *systemic* solutions to your problem. Hold the systems in your care—or at least subject to your charm and influence—wholly and radically accountable for their outcomes. When we wrote about this challenge in our first book, we named the chapter "It's Not Your

---

*Note that these slides have still not been updated.

Employees' Fault."[14] In it we describe a frustrating service hotline experience, something most of us deal with on a weekly basis. We point out that the exasperating service rep is probably watching up to eight screens at once while trying to assist customers from all cultures, ages, and levels of expertise with an exploding range of product and service needs. Given typical investments in salary and training, that person is either an effective communicator without the ability to solve technical problems or a competent technician with limited interpersonal skills. Neither one can reliably help you.

The "bad guy" in this performance failure, of course, isn't the overwhelmed and underskilled service rep. It's the system this employee was dropped into—a system that sets people up to fail. We like to quote former Secretary of Veterans Affairs Robert McDonald, who often pointed out that "organizations are perfectly designed to get the results they get. . . . if you don't like the results, you need to change the design." A thirty-plus-year veteran of Procter & Gamble, where he ultimately served as CEO and chairman, McDonald took a holistic approach to solving problems that allowed him to move fast and fix things at a sprawling, change-resistant Department of Veterans Affairs. Instead of blaming employees, he held the environment in which they worked wholly and radically accountable.[15]

Even if a part of you thinks the solution to your problem is to find better people (we'll go there next) or that the people you have simply need to try harder (we'll also go *there*), suspend your disbelief. For now, take your employees off the table as an explanatory variable and experiment with all the *other* parts of the system that may be responsible for your problem. As you start

SOLVE FOR TRUST   65

to investigate, consider that you may be operating with inherited norms, structures, and divisions of labor that were designed for a different moment in your organization's history—or a different organization entirely. There's no rule, for example, that says you must have stable teams or only one CEO or frontline workers with fewer decision rights than their bosses.

Old-school bookseller Barnes & Noble recently found its competitive footing again *against Amazon* by giving its store managers license to customize the service experience and product mix, a fairly radical departure for large retailers. "I get all the glory," CEO James Daunt reflected, "but actually what I'm doing is getting out of people's way and letting them run decent bookstores."[16] Be willing to bring Daunt-like skepticism to any operating choice your organization has made, no matter how long you've been making it or how many of your competitors are doing the same things.

You don't even need *titles* for your new ways of working, not if it doesn't make sense for the business. When Gusto, the highly rated HR platform (think payroll, benefits, etc., all in one place), experimented with replacing job titles with functional descriptions, Jessica Huen, the company's head of people at the time, explained the decision this way: "We had a lot of internal discussions. Does it matter if we say a role is senior or junior? Do we have to differentiate at this stage between a backend and frontend developer?"[17]

In response to the change, Huen saw an expansion in the range of talent applying to roles: "Our hiring managers are seeing incredible people come through—people who never would've applied before because all the titles were preventing them from taking the leap."[18] But the more interesting impact of the change was cultural. "Going titleless has also impacted us on a psychological level," Huen added. "Now someone isn't a senior customer care advocate; they're simply on the care team. That slight shift in wording captures the collaborative nature of what we're trying to accomplish here." Take it from Huen: at this point in the development of your Good Enough Plan, you have a mandate to question *everything*.

> **GUT CHECK:** Proceed when you're willing to hold the design of your organization responsible for its outcomes.

Identify "New" Talent

A third major trust unlock is to find new people with the skills to solve your problem, and we suggest starting the search close to home. Before looking for talent outside the business, make sure you're not overlooking someone on your team who may be ready to take the ball. As LinkedIn CEO Ryan Roslansky put it recently, "Your next best employee is most likely your current employee."[19]

This is the part of your plan we'll call *advancement* experiments, which includes any new ideas you have for increasing merit-based mobility inside the company. Advancement is a reliable logic bet that delivers better outcomes than hiring externally: more often than not, outside hires perform worse on the job, leave their post sooner, and cost more.[20] Advancement also has powerful empathy externalities since it broadcasts to everyone that employees are vital stakeholders. *You see our centrality and value us accordingly.*

Companies that excel at advancement have well-functioning internal talent markets, which is harder than it sounds to pull off. Think transparent, rigorous processes for internal recruitment and selection. Think cultures that are defined by active sponsorship, where people are championing other people, even when they're not in the room. Think proactive rewards systems, where employees are progressively compensated for their growing contributions to the business without having to lobby for recognition or play hardball by soliciting external offers.

Don't think lowballing your current employees on comp but stretching to pay a premium for shiny, external hires. *Don't* think cultures where opportunity flows to whomever maneuvers politically for it. *Don't* think open positions that are filled de facto before you post the job (meaning after you've essentially already found your person).* By the way, companies regularly underestimate how much cynicism this behavior breeds and how deflating it can be for the people who participate in what ends up feeling like sham hiring theater.

Even when you've led a good-faith internal search, there's risk that a hiring process destroys more trust than it builds. One way to reduce this risk is to give candidates robust feedback on why they *didn't* get a job. That's what Mignon Early, vice president of DEI at Fresenius Medical Care, did when she designed a pilot program to turn rejecting internal candidates—a painful moment in any organization—into a learning opportunity. When

---

*In our experience, this rarely happens explicitly or fraudulently, but the cultural costs of the behavior are the same.

Early posted jobs for a new function she was building, sixty internal candidates applied for three open positions, many of them bringing exciting perspectives and skills to the role. Her hiring team met with every internal candidate they passed on to explain why they didn't get the job and engage them on career goals, development plans, and interest in other open positions at the company.

In reflecting on the pilot, Early told us, "We went from bracing ourselves for the fallout of our decision to having very real conversations with so many great people about their futures and career goals." Some of them ended up becoming ambassadors for Early's team. "Their experience was ultimately positive, and they also really got what we're trying to build here." Early's pilot highlights a perpetually missed opportunity in recruitment and promotions: although far more people are being rejected than accepted, many of them colleagues who will remain an important part of your ecosystem, companies often spend little time thinking through the mechanics and signaling of that rejection.*

Advancement, done well, also ensures that you're not overlooking colleagues with an overly sticky "potential" label. Comedian and actress Tiffany Haddish has made "she ready" a professional anthem, even using it in the names of her production company and foundation. Haddish's talent was overlooked at various points in her career, despite her ability to dominate some of the biggest stages in the world.[21] When we find ourselves in talent meetings, we often hear Haddish's voice as a challenge to make sure no one is being counted out too quickly or casually

---

*We often see this same algorithm of missed opportunity in early-stage investing, membership organizations, and up-or-out talent cultures.

labeled as "not quite ready for prime time." More than once we've used the phrase as shorthand to each other when we see capacity in someone the rest of the room isn't seeing.

You may decide that you genuinely *can't* promote from within— just be sure to make this call with sufficient rigor. Claire Hughes Johnson, former COO of Stripe (and current corporate officer and adviser), uses a five-step decision-making matrix before deciding on an outside search, a tool that's begging to be piloted inside your own organization. For context, Hughes Johnson helped to grow Stripe from fewer than two hundred employees to more than six thousand—and from millions in revenues to *billions*. At various points in her move-fast-and-fix-it tenure, she led business operations, sales, marketing, customer support, risk management, and all of Stripe's people functions. Whatever problem you're tackling this week, Hughes Johnson has probably solved some variation of it. In evaluating internal talent for advancement, the questions she challenges leaders to reflect on include, "Can I or others at the company support and help develop this person to learn the job in the next six months?" Only when you consistently answer no do you earn a Hughes Johnson–endorsed "Great! Hire externally."*

External recruiting is another business process that's ripe for experimentation. The objective of external recruiting is to get good at hiring *people you don't already know* (more on this challenge tomorrow), meaning people who bring new networks, influences, and life experiences to the company. To break out of its own hiring rut, one experiment Stripe ran was a coding

---

*Hughes Johnson has decided to share these questions and 446 additional pages of insight in her book *Scaling People*, which is a nuanced operating manual for anyone growing a business ambitiously. If you're looking for experiments to run at this point in the story, we invite you to pick any page in her book for inspiration.

competition called Capture the Flag, which generated industry buzz and exposed the company to exceptional developers they *didn't already know.* The inaugural event attracted 12,000 unique visitors, 250 of whom figured out how to capture the flag. All 12,000 were new beeps in human form—and 250 became high-value targets for the company's expanding hiring pipeline.[22]

> **GUT CHECK:** Proceed when you know which capabilities you're missing—and whether the only way to source them is to hire externally.

Make the Difficult People Decisions

Over the past decade, we've worked with countless senior executives, many of them in challenging circumstances. Regret is rarely an emotion we see, but when it does show up, it's almost always regret at not moving fast enough to let go of someone who was no longer right for the company. This section is less about running smart experiments and more about getting over the barriers to taking smart action. In virtually every organization we've advised, there's been a difficult people decision that leaders were hesitating to make. Tuesday is an invitation to finally make it.

The ability to gracefully part ways with employees is among your most important tactical leadership skills. In *Unleashed*, we offer guidance on how to do this in a way that honors the dignity of the people being let go, in everything from the separation package to the timing and location of the discussion.[23] We point out that while it has somehow become standard practice to make separated employees feel like criminals, the retaliation risk rarely justifies the humiliation we extract on their way out the door. These choices are investments in empathy for the person at the center of the separation story, but you're also making it clear to everyone else that no one gets dehumanized on your watch.

Separations *can* build trust at the company level by communicating clarity of business needs (logic), willingness to defend whatever performance bar you've set (authenticity), and an *unwillingness* to tolerate unproductive behavior (empathy). But separation decisions—and their clumsy execution—often end up destroying more trust than they build. For example, the research is clear that badly executed and/or badly motivated layoffs rarely help senior leaders accomplish their goals. Although it may *feel* like progress, layoffs can be a counterintuitive drag on key performance metrics, including profitability. Among the biggest drivers are lower job satisfaction and higher flight of remaining employees, including your best people.[24]

As we write this, the tech industry is offering the world a robust education in these high-stakes dynamics. The sector is now riding waves of layoffs after hiring prodigiously during the demand peaks of pandemic living. Since many of these decisions appear logical to shareholders, the market is rewarding companies shedding workers with higher stock prices. But with the layoff research as a touch point, we find ourselves skeptical about the impact of some of these decisions. In our experience, the path to Accelerating Excellence is not littered with layoff announcements.

How do layoffs fit into your larger change strategy? How do they connect the company from its current challenges to its future success? These are the same questions you'll be asked by your best employees, the ones you need to stick around to achieve that future. On Thursday, we'll explore the importance and mechanics of change storytelling, and we'll offer as a preview that reducing your ranks in a material way is a major company decision, one that needs a story, even in moments like now, when everyone else is doing it.

Finally, a few notes on separating from employees who are doing damage, culturally or otherwise. First, make sure your analysis is correct. We worked with one team that was quick to label as "toxic" a new employee (we'll call her Anita) who was deviating from the company's relatively narrow standard of conflict-averse behavior. Instead of changing the way their new colleague showed up in the workplace, it was in the company's best interest at this point in its trajectory to adopt some of Anita's scrappy, competitive energy.

When you're confident in your assessment of true harm, move quickly. We often say that organizational change can fix good people behaving badly, but it can't fix bad people behaving badly—employees with an established pattern of malice, discrimination, or misconduct. We believe that your only defensible option for the latter category is to separate those employees from the company. In our experience, there aren't very many of these people roaming our organizational halls, but they can do tremendous harm at individual, team, and organizational levels.

To be clear, we're not ruling out anyone's rehabilitation, but it doesn't need to happen on your watch if there's been a high personal and cultural price for someone's behavior. The cost of dehumanizing others—at a minimum—must be giving up the privilege of being around them. Again, determining who's in this camp requires a good, fair, transparent process, as well as institutional confidence in the outcomes of that process. Pitchfork justice helps nobody.

> **GUT CHECK:** Proceed when you have clarity on whom to let go—and a plan for doing it in a way that builds more trust than it destroys.

Don't Make It All about You

Empathy is the company wobble we're seeing most frequently these days. When anxiety is on the march, empathy tends to retreat—and these are anxious times. It's hard to focus on other people when we have parts inside us shouting about threats to our own survival.* (By the way, it's not that their threat assessment is necessarily wrong; it's that self-distraction isn't going to get you very far.)

We've pushed this section to the back end of the chapter because empathy wobbles tend to present very passionately, often in the form of aggrieved customers or frustrated employees pointing out all the ways the company has disappointed them. And while they've earned the right to demand your attention, their passion can also obscure other problems that may be at the root of the company's wobbling empathy. If systems are perfectly designed to get the results they get, then something

---

*Hi, Uncle Dick!

systematic may be getting in the way of being responsive to the needs of a given stakeholder.

At a minimum, something systematic is going to be part of the solution, so we want you to show up for this part of your Good Enough Plan with deep understanding of your operating strengths and weaknesses, particularly when it comes to your people—*all of them.* We worked with one hospital system whose outside physicians were tired of being treated like second-class citizens. They were an essential part of the patient care team, and yet they had limited access to basic tools such as complete patient records. Getting to a solution started with challenging the company's beliefs about who these doctors were, including the flawed assumption that they were mercenaries who put money over mission (in truth, most were entrepreneurial personalities who were energized by the challenge of building their own practice). But we quickly moved from mental models to very practical pilot solutions, which were all in the category of more graceful operations: inclusive IT systems, a visitor's badge process that wasn't cumbersome, a place to store their stuff and take phone calls when they were on-site. These changes dramatically shifted the team's interpersonal dynamics.

We started you on logic interventions to help improve your wobble response time. The currency of empathy is often capability improvements that allow you to better meet the needs of whichever stakeholder is being undervalued. When Uber set out to steady its empathy wobbles with employees, drivers, and riders, the smart experiments the company ran started with an overhaul of its values that led with "We Do the Right Thing. Period," an unambiguous empathy signal that it wasn't going to be all about the company going forward. But the rest of the ideas came from the logic side of the ledger: new driver-tipping functionality, new passenger safety features, investments in better HR processes.[25]

Talk directly with the people who have decided that it's all about you, even if it means revisiting some Monday activities. Work to understand their perspective, on both the foundations of problems and the architecture of potential solutions. Resist the temptation to skip this step because it's obvious what a stakeholder needs from you. Activist and icon Gloria Steinem often tells a story about her encounter with a turtle when she was a reluctant geology student at Smith College.* Having wandered away from a lecture on the banks of the Connecticut River, Steinem discovered a confused turtle far from the river and diligently returned it to its aquatic habitat (the story is about to get more exciting). "Just as I had slipped it into the water and was watching it swim away, my geology professor came up behind me. 'You know,' he said quietly, 'that turtle has probably spent a month crawling up the dirt path to lay its eggs in the mud on the side of the road.'" Steinem felt terrible, of course, but didn't internalize the leadership lesson until she started down the path of becoming a global changemaker: "It took me many more years to realize this parable had taught me the first rule of organizing. Always ask the turtle."[26]

Companies that excel at empathy are in active dialogue with their "turtles" (read: stakeholders) and often have good wobble-detection systems in place. Chobani founder and CEO Hamdi

---

*Frances, I couldn't find anywhere else to work animals into the manuscript.

Ulukaya built a global yogurt empire by keeping customers at the center of the business, both operationally and culturally. One experiment that Ulukaya ran in the company's early days was to put his own phone number on yogurt containers so that customers could call him directly with feedback.[27] But it was what happened next that made the difference on empathy. Ulukaya succeeded wildly because when the phone rang, he was riveted by what the person on the other end of the line had to say to him.

> **GUT CHECK:** Proceed when you've identified the stakeholders who aren't convinced that the organization genuinely cares about them.

Walk the Talk

In 2022 outdoor clothing brand Patagonia declared that "Earth is now our only shareholder." The statement explained a formal transfer of ownership from founder Yvon Chouinard to two new entities (one trust, one not-for-profit) whose collective raison d'être was to aggressively fight the climate crisis. In this new experimental structure, all profits not reinvested in the business—projected to be about $100 million annually—would be used to fund organizations and activities that directly protected the planet. "Instead of extracting value from nature and transforming it into wealth," Chouinard explained, "we are using the wealth Patagonia creates to protect the source. . . . I am dead serious about saving this planet."[28]

Chouinard did not need to clarify how serious he was. The world already knew. Patagonia has consistently topped the list of the most trusted brands in American business.[29] The company has not achieved this distinction because its values are universally shared, but because those values have been unshakably aligned with the bold decisions it has made as a business for almost forty years. Now generating over $1 billion in annual sales, the company has donated 1 percent of all revenues back to environmental groups since 1985. It has often been first and best in using recycled materials, protecting labor rights, and reducing the environmental impact of its manufacturing processes. Its stores and offices are regularly closed so that employees can do things that are more important to the fate of the planet than their day jobs, things like voting on election day. The company even sued the US government for misuse of public lands.[30]

The lack of daylight between Patagonia's words and actions is one of the best corporate examples we know of *authenticity* at scale. Yes, the company competes rigorously on *logic* (see revenue curve, up and to the right) and reveals deep *empathy* (see radically graceful returns processes) for its customers, employees, and suppliers, but what drives consumers' outsize trust in Patagonia is its willingness to authentically walk its environmental talk. The company simply *is* who it says it is and *does* what it says it will do. Full stop.

Keep Chouinard in the back of your mind as you hunt down authenticity wobbles in your own organization and make fixing them part of your Good Enough Plan.[31] They often present as a lack of alignment between something you've literally said to a stakeholder and your ability (read: willingness) to fully deliver on it. Social media companies often end up at the bottom of the lists that Patagonia tops because of the industry's pattern of loudly asserting one thing and then doing something else entirely, such as claiming that the rules apply to all and then tolerating violations from high-profile users.[32] But these kinds of breaks can also present in less dramatic ways, such as when your marketing team exaggerates your product claims. They're often derivative of mundane organizational problems like poor communication or conflict aversion.

In our work we often reflect on Hanlon's razor: *never attribute to malice that which is adequately explained by neglect.** People who invoke this maxim sometimes replace the word *neglect* with *incompetence* or *stupidity*, but those are unnecessarily judgy words. In our experience, neglect is the right editorial choice because most company authenticity wobbles are explained by process breakdowns or sloppy collaboration between different parts of the business. And while no one's intentions may have been bad, this isn't how your skeptical stakeholders will see it.

The problem is that it just *feels bad* to be on the receiving end of an authenticity wobble. United Airlines recently made the news for misplacing a savvy passenger's checked bag. The traveler had placed an Apple AirTag inside her bag to hedge against feeling powerless in precisely this scenario, and so she knew she was getting bad information from the airline's rep, who assured

---

*For our readers with more interesting hobbies than words: *razor* is a philosophical term to describe a theory of human behavior. This particular razor is attributed to a man named Robert Hanlon from Scranton, Pennsylvania, but someone named *Heinlen* may have also made this observation a few decades earlier. We've learned to never bet against Scranton, so we're giving Hanlon full credit.

her that the company had everything under control. As United urged the frustrated passenger to calm down, she was tracking her bag in real time to a McDonald's, a suburban shopping center, and ultimately to a random apartment complex.[33]

The passenger documented her ordeal on Twitter and finally tweeted out, exasperated, "I'd just like everyone to know that @ united has lost track of my bag and is lying about it." She finally got her bag back, but since conspiracies are good for ratings, the story ends with two television news crews showing up at the random apartment complex—and with anyone following the story wondering how much they could trust United Airlines. Meanwhile, this service failure was likely preventable with better communication systems and more active supplier management, business processes that are often begging for more active experimentation. In United's statement about the incident, the company explained that "the service our baggage delivery vendor provided does not meet our standards." We've been doing this work long enough to know that this was unlikely to be the first time those standards were not met.

Don't wait for news crews to show up to figure out where you're collectively saying one thing and then doing another. Throw everything you've got at finding your authenticity wobbles and running smart experiments in how to steady them, including piloting ways to change an organizational culture that's revealed a willingness to tolerate them. Tomorrow we'll talk more about creating the space for *individual* authenticity—also known as inclusion—but for now, prioritize repairing the mechanics of any systemic authenticity breaks. Take a stand for making sure that the *company* says what it means and means what it says.

Finally, celebrate the progress you've made today. If you've done even a fraction of what we've proposed, then your Good Enough Plan is now an Even Better Plan. Remember those adult beverages on your packing list? You have our blessing to break them out now and reflect on the wisdom of Jim Koch, legendary cofounder and chairman of the Boston Beer Company, who is widely seen as the father of the American craft brewing movement (there's a good chance that Koch invented the beverage you're holding in your hand). When we asked Koch about his company's dramatic ascent, he said, "We treated the right kind of failure as perfectly acceptable." The work of Tuesday is to embrace this mindset and see how much trust you can build as you go.

> **GUT CHECK:** Proceed when you've solved for trust.

WEDNESDAY

Make New Friends

Whatever problem you're tackling this week, you're going to be better at solving it with people who don't already think like you do—people with different perspectives, different assumptions, different experiences of moving through the world. You've heard this before, we know, but today is your chance to practice. On Wednesday, you'll improve your Even Better Plan by tapping into the full humanity of your team. The theme of the day is *inclusion*.

Inclusion is the act of creating conditions for other people to thrive, not in spite of their differences as complex, multidimensional humans, but precisely *because* of those differences. It's the ultimate investment in organizational trust because it accelerates all three trust drivers at once: when team members can bring their individual differences to work, the team is more capable of meeting stakeholder needs with rigorous logic, deep empathy, and high authenticity and *less* capable of the kinds of trust wobbles we explored yesterday—the unforced errors that take real time to circle back to and clean up. Inclusion creates a flywheel of trust that allows you to do everything else faster and better.

In all the flux and churn of the DEI debate, this is the part of the story that sometimes gets muddled: inclusion helps you *win*.* Among other payoffs, inclusion makes us smarter, more innovative, and more profitable. Inclusion increases our collective access to knowledge, which enables us to see our competitive landscape more clearly. Inclusion delivers all of this (and more!) without hiring lots of new people or investing in expensive technology. (See "Ten Delicious Findings on the Competitive Advantages of Inclusion"). No other organizational upgrade you're contemplating can compete with those kinds of returns, which is why we're going to spend a full "day" on the topic, even if you haven't identified it as an urgent problem. Wherever you're aiming on the FIX map, inclusion will catapult you closer to your destination.

This doesn't mean inclusion is easy to pull off. The other part of the story that sometimes gets confused is the inconvenient truth that building an inclusive organization takes effort. You can't throw a diverse group of people together and hope for the best.** In fact, this often makes things worse. Diverse teams reliably underperform homogenous teams unless you first do the

---

*Some have argued, persuasively, that the ethical imperatives of inclusion should be enough to justify investment in it. Our view is a practical, both/and perspective rooted in assumptions we've seen get in the way of sustainable culture change. When inclusion is seen solely as a moral good, without taking into account its full value as a competitive asset, it often fails to receive sufficient organizational resources and attention.

**"Hope for the best" can sometimes present as launching a few Employee Resource Groups and hosting an unconscious-bias training.

WEDNESDAY'S AGENDA

1. Figure out why you're doing this.

2. Find your place(s) on the Inclusion Dial.

3. Make it physically and emotionally safe to be different.

4. Make it *psychologically* safe to be different.

5. Welcome everyone despite their differences.

6. Celebrate uniqueness on your own team.

7. Champion uniqueness at the scale of the organization.

8. Include yourself, too.

Materials You'll Need for Today

- Open mind

- Survey software

- Energy and confidence to improve things, also known (*casual*) as can-do lesbian spirit

- Willingness to let go of whatever assumptions you've reached about inclusion based on the utility of your last DEI workshop

- Experience being a complex, multidimensional person

---

work to make those teams inclusive (we explore why in the next section). That's the bad news. The good news is that when you do that work, inclusive teams end up, to use a technical term, *thumping* everyone else. They may move more slowly in the short term, but they make up the speed over time and produce consistently better outcomes.[1]

Kevin Nolan, CEO of GE Appliances, put it this way as he reflected on his own campaign to build a company that could compete and win on inclusion: "Diversity is uncomfortable. I think it's been sold in corporate trainings like it's going to be nirvana. It's not. It's going to be more uncomfortable. But you're going to get better results." In our experience, Nolan is right, which is why organizations need a very clear *why* to push through the discomfort.

One way to motivate the power of inclusion is to indulge the counterfactual. What if a more inclusive team had been calling the shots? Would we have fixed more things—or, at minimum, broken fewer? Kara Swisher, legendary tech journalist and can-do lesbian (our greatest compliment), thinks that the internet, for one, would be a better place. Swisher has observed that "far too many of the people who have designed the wondrous parts of the internet—thinking up cool new products to make our lives easier, distributing them across the globe and making fortunes doing so—have never felt unsafe a day in their lives."[2] We're now experiencing what happens when the people in charge of guardrails have no idea what it feels like to rely on them.

What if things had been different? What if, to use Swisher's example, more tech companies were led by more people who have felt a twinge of fear getting into a stranger's car or been harassed in the workplace or felt afraid or even just out of place because of some aspect of their identity? We're confident we wouldn't be patching so much software that fails to anticipate so many harms. We're confident we wouldn't be building so many grand councils to issue after-the-fact edicts on user behavior. We're confident we *would* be living in a different world, a better world, for all of us, one that's designed for the reality of being a sometimes-vulnerable human, which is the experience so many of us endure.

Guess who gets to build that different, better world? The answer is you, glorious you. Welcome to Wednesday.

Figure Out Why You're Doing This

For the absence of doubt, it's not just underrepresented employees who benefit from getting inclusion right. We are *all* better off in inclusive spaces where we can bring a more authentic version of ourselves to work. We feel better, build more trust, and are more likely to contribute our unique stores of knowledge, information, and experience.

That last one—the unique contribution part—turns out to be a big deal from a performance standpoint.* Getting people to share what they know *that other people don't know* is the key to, well, a whole lot of this winning thing. This pattern is explained by something called the *common information effect*, which sounds benign and technical but should be entering our story accompanied by scary music and other clues to its pernicious effects.[3]

The dreaded common information effect works like this: As human beings, we tend to focus on the things we have *in common* with other people. We seek out and affirm the knowledge we share, as it signals our value and kinship with the group.** In diverse teams, by definition, this instinct limits the amount

---

*One of our favorite exercises to do with MBA students is a simulation designed by Amy Edmondson and Mike Roberto where teams must figure out how to survive at the top of Mt. Everest. Teams that report higher feelings of group belonging consistently outperform other teams for the simple reason that individuals are more willing to share what they uniquely know.

**This makes good evolutionary sense since our survival depended on that kinship.

FIGURE 3-1

Available information for diverse and homogeneous teams

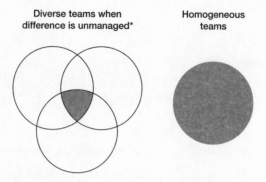

Diverse teams when
difference is unmanaged*

Homogeneous
teams

*The common information effect focuses a team on shared knowledge and limits access to unique information.

Source: Frances Frei and Anne Morriss, *Unleashed: The Unapologetic Leader's Guide to Empowering Everyone Around You* (Boston: Harvard Business Review Press, 2020).

of information that's available for collective decision-making. Diverse teams simply have less shared knowledge to work with, which explains the performance gap we mentioned at the beginning of the chapter. Diverse teams often underperform homogenous teams if we let the common information effect run its course.

Figure 3-1 illustrates how this dynamic plays out for two teams of three people (the circles are meant to be the people). On the first team, the three teammates are different from each other and their shared knowledge is represented by where the circles overlap. On the second team, where the three teammates are so similar that they're stacked on top of each other, their shared knowledge is represented by the entire circle.

But here's what makes inclusion so critical to your performance: it *cancels* the common information effect. Inclusion gives us access to everyone's unique information, not just the

FIGURE 3-2

Available information for inclusive teams

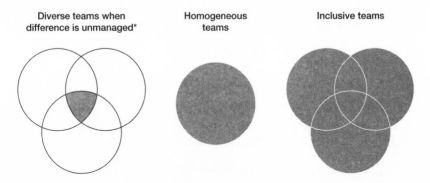

Diverse teams when difference is unmanaged*

Homogeneous teams

Inclusive teams

*The common information effect focuses a team on shared knowledge and limits access to unique information.

Source: Frances Frei and Anne Morriss, *Unleashed: The Unapologetic Leader's Guide to Empowering Everyone Around You* (Boston: Harvard Business Review Press, 2020).

information we happen to share. When we build teams that are both diverse and inclusive, teams that value everyone's unique, multidimensional selves, we get to *expand* the amount of information the team can access. Organizations start to look a lot more like figure 3-2, where an inclusive three-person team has what it needs to thump the other two teams.

This is why the distinction between diversity and inclusion is so meaningful. In our experience, many teams working toward inclusion are getting stuck at the diversity stage—recruiting difference without managing it effectively—and generating frustration and cynicism about their own DEI efforts along the way. They're effectively stopping in the middle of the change journey and declaring failure prematurely.

When inclusion researchers Randall Peterson and Heidi Gardner explored the distinction between diversity and inclusion on boards of directors, it was inclusion—not just diversity—that boosted performance, including higher stock prices.[4] But getting there takes work and time. Peterson and Gardner's counsel on how to speed things up resonates with our own experience, including the value of leaders who know how to listen and the impact of proactively reaching across identity boundaries.

We'll explore a practical, move-fast-and-fix-things approach to inclusion for the rest of the day, but we want to start by inviting you to get in touch with the *systemic* value of this effort. Wednesday is not just about taking care of a subset of your employees, the X's on a team filled with Y's, although that's an important part of it (particularly if those X's are disengaged and undervalued). Wednesday is about everybody else, too. Dennis Brockman, global chief inclusion and diversity officer at Starbucks, often finds himself clarifying this point: "Something I say a lot, that's important to understand, is that inclusion does not mean exclusion. This work is not only about our BIPOC partners. This work is about how we want every partner to have an opportunity to be included in this organization."[5] Brockman has identified the motivating fact of today's work: the *whole* organization is better off in the presence of full inclusion—and much worse off in its absence.

This also means that it's our shared moral and competitive imperative to create workplaces where the challenges and opportunities of inclusion are shouldered by everyone, not only by the so-called diverse. As our friend Bozoma Saint John, among the planet's most effective, in-the-trenches changemakers, has said to us, "Why do I, as a Black woman, have to fix it all? There are way more of you than there are of me. We need some help out here."

Ten Delicious Findings on the Competitive Advantages of Inclusion

Although it can be hard to measure a complex outcome like inclusion, researchers are getting better at it. Serious people are working to identify and quantify the many effects of inclusion on firm performance, and the insights they're generating are persuasive. Below is a list of some of our favorite findings, many of which remain generally underappreciated.

1. **Inclusion helps you recruit good people.** Inclusion is now a tell for all kinds of talented people—not only the underrepresented—that you've built a healthy workplace and understand what it takes to collectively excel. Expect candidates to look for evidence of inclusiveness in everything from where you recruit to the fine print of your benefits package. For example, they may not need those same-sex fertility benefits or veteran mentorship services, but they'll still see them as a sign that you appreciate difference.[7]

2. **Inclusion helps you retain good people.** It turns out that those same candidates will stick around as employees if you truly walk the talk on inclusion. Inclusion drives higher rates of retention at all levels of the organization, and some employee segments (military veterans top the list) will reward your ability to value their unique contribution with industry-leading loyalty.[8]

3. **Inclusion increases the engagement of your people.** Engagement scores are consistently higher for companies labeled "inclusive," and we now have some interesting data that helps to explain these numbers.

(continued)

Inclusive companies are *also* almost three times better at coaching people for improved performance and four times better at identifying and building leaders. Making people better is the key to their engagement, and inclusion seems to give you an advantage.[9]

4. **Inclusion makes you more resilient.** When different types of people are thriving in your organization, you're better at navigating crises and (our favorite business euphemism) "turbulent times" in general. You're more adaptable, more comfortable with change, and better at dealing with personnel problems.[10] One fun fact: while the S&P saw a 35 percent decline in stock performance between 2007 and 2009 (remember that ride?), the shares of inclusive companies went in the other direction, gaining over 14 percent in value.[11]

5. **Inclusion grows your marketplace.** Inclusive teams are better at identifying and cultivating new markets because they expand a firm's peripheral vision and help eliminate its blind spots.[12] More women in decision-making roles, for example, improves a company's ability to solve problems for female clients.[13] And this is before we even get to the macro implications of *economic* inclusion. For example, the US GDP could get a boost of up to $25 billion if just 1 percent more of persons with disabilities joined the labor force.[14] What percentage of that boost would represent new customers for your business?

6. **Inclusion makes you more innovative.** Inclusion creates a healthier meritocracy for new ideas where out-of-the-box thinking is more likely to break through.[15] This happens in part because people in inclusive organizations are more likely to surface and hear the *what* of a good idea rather

than allow that idea to be diluted or buried by an unexpected *who*. How much of an innovation bump does true inclusion buy you? Depending on your starting place, estimates range from roughly 20 percent all the way up to 70 percent.[16]

7. **Inclusion turns you into better decision-makers.** Decision quality goes up when a range of voices are not only present but also integrated.[17] In one delightful study, all-male teams beat individuals nearly 60 percent of the time, but gender-diverse teams outperformed individuals almost 75 percent of the time. Teams that were gender diverse, geographically diverse, and had at least one age gap of more than twenty years made better decisions than that lone individual *87 percent of the time.*[18]

8. **Inclusion helps you manage risk.** In the wreckage of the 2008 financial crisis, a serious "Lehman Sisters" argument emerged positing that the story would have played out differently if more women had been in the room for the most consequential decisions. Subsequent studies have since explored this argument, concluding that gender inclusion in the C-suite and boardroom is associated with a healthier firm relationship to risk—neither overly risk-averse nor risk-seeking—and better overall performance.[19]

9. **Inclusion improves your stock price.** Estimated bumps to shareholder returns range from 10 percent to over 30 percent (seriously) when you get inclusion right.[20] This may be why Goldman Sachs recently announced that it would no longer take any company public where the board is made up exclusively of straight, white men.[21] Whatever your organization's own return on inclusion may

(continued)

end up being, the question we often ask companies is, "What else are you doing to chase those kinds of returns?"

10. **Inclusion makes you more money.** For all the reasons we've covered in entries 1–9, inclusion ends up boosting both your top line and bottom line. Your talented, engaged teams will drive higher revenues through better innovation and smarter market development, while allowing you to spend capital more efficiently through better decision-making, higher retention, and higher productivity. And when you hit some turbulence along the way, you're more likely to land the plane safely. We hope to live in a world where inclusion is an organizational given. Until we get there, we know of no other distinction that can deliver these kinds of advantages.[22]

We have the day together to answer Saint John's call, but the punch line is that it's not as hard as it may seem. As we've written about before, inclusion is an urgent, achievable goal that requires far less audacity than disrupting industries or growing complex organizations—things companies do every day without fear and confusion shutting down progress.

When Intel CEO Pat Gelsinger was recently asked why his company was spending so much time on DEI, he had a fast answer: "Diversity, equity, and inclusion accelerate innovation, attract top talent, deepen employee engagement, and improve the bottom line."[6] In our experience, that kind of clarity, particularly at the top of an organization, can be enormously helpful in getting all the way to a culture of full inclusion—and to the Accelerating Excellence it enables. So why are *you* doing this work?

> **GUT CHECK:** Proceed when you've clarified
> your own organization's case for inclusion.

Find Your Place(s) on the Inclusion Dial

We're going to kick off the day with a good, old-fashioned review of terms. A culture of inclusion has four levels: safe, welcome, celebrated, and championed. We think about these distinctions in the following way:

1. *Safe.* People feel physically, emotionally, and psychologically safe in the workplace, regardless of who they are.

2. *Welcome.* People feel welcome in the workplace throughout the entire HR life cycle, regardless of who they are; they can bring an authentic version of themselves to shared workspaces without penalty.

3. *Celebrated.* People feel celebrated in the workplace *because of* who they are; they are rewarded for contributing their unique information, ideas, and perspectives to advance the organization's goals.

4. *Championed.* A culture of inclusion permeates the organization; inclusion is seen as an ethical and competitive imperative, and there is minimal variability in the experience of belonging across individuals, teams, and functions.

As an organization moves up the Inclusion Dial, its ambitions grow from ensuring that people are safe and welcome *in spite of* their differences to ensuring they're valued—celebrated and championed—*because of* their uniqueness. Again, this is good for (checks notes) *everyone*. When you're high up on the Inclusion Dial, the common information effect doesn't stand a chance.

The dial's levels are progressive in the sense that welcome is more inclusive than safe, and so on. You also can't skip over one level to get to the next.* For example, Frances was once invited to give a talk in a country with laws that are quite hostile to LGBTQ+ people like us. When she declined, citing safety concerns, she was assured that the red carpet would be rolled out in spite of who she is. But her hosts could have thrown her a parade and given speeches in her honor, and she still wouldn't have gotten on that plane. No amount of welcome can make up for the absence of safety.

Since we're wildly competitive and grew up on game shows like *Press Your Luck*, we cannot resist using a picture of an oversize dial to show you how all this works (see figure 3-3).

(Yes, you win when you get all the way to championed.)

Where on the Inclusion Dial are you and your colleagues? Get out that survey software we asked you to bring today and measure the inclusiveness of your own team. Anonymously survey your immediate team members and at least one other team in the company (more data is more in this case). We suggest you keep things simple and ask a single, inclusion-related question:

---

*You will hear echoes of Maslow's famous hierarchy of needs in the progression of the Inclusion Dial. Maslow's ultimate goal of self-actualization can be achieved in organizations, we believe, when the things that make us different as people are recognized and valued.

FIGURE 3-3

The Inclusion Dial

Source: Frances Frei and Anne Morriss, *Unleashed: The Unapologetic Leader's Guide to Empowering Everyone Around You* (Boston: Harvard Business Review Press, 2020).

Which word best describes your experience of inclusion at work?

A.   None of the below (i.e., not yet safe)

B.   Safe

C.   Welcome

D.   Celebrated

E.   Championed

You're welcome to also collect basic profile information (demographics, rank, function, etc.), but only if you can credibly protect the anonymity of respondents and eliminate any possibility of retaliation.

Here's what will happen next: you will get back a range of answers, which is often eye-opening to leaders when we do this work with them. The distribution of responses is often wide and startlingly stable across teams and organizations, even among employees at the top of a hierarchy. About 40 percent of people feel welcome at work, and roughly 30 percent feel either celebrated or championed. The most surprising result to many of our partners is that a material percentage of respondents tops out at safe, and *some of your colleagues don't even feel safe when they come to work.* We're going to urge you to focus first on this last segment—people experiencing the absence of safety—with the clarity and speed of someone whose teammates are in harm's way, because they very well may be (we'll get started in the next section).

If you did gather profile information, you're likely to see trends in who lands where on the Inclusion Dial, patterns that will inform the work you do today. If you're like most organizations, for example, some identities, teams, and/or functions are more likely than others to feel a deep sense of belonging. Although not everyone in a particular group will be having the same inclusion experience, notice the directional patterns. How do these patterns inform the problem you set out to solve on Monday?

Your inclusion data will help to organize and motivate today's work. An important outcome of this exercise is to get in touch with the fact that if you're like most organizations, then you're not yet realizing the full potential of an inclusive workplace (recall those ten delicious findings).* Even those of you in the high-trust quadrants of our FIX map are likely to have room for improvement. If you needed any additional motivation for today, let this data be your fuel.

We're going to spend the rest of the day working to move *everyone* on your team up the Inclusion Dial, starting with the

---

*Another thing that many organizations take away from this exercise is that they don't have great listening systems in place for understanding the day-to-day experience of their people. Even companies that are excellent at taking the pulse of their customers are often in the relative dark about what it feels like to be an employee.

essential work of ensuring that your people, at a minimum, feel safe on the job by the standards of your shared profession. We'll then work on how to move people from safe to welcome, from welcome to celebrated, and ultimately from celebrated to championed. Finally, we'll end the day by exploring how to show up authentically and value your own unique contribution without having to wait for other people to get this right.

One operating note: we'll be working on moving people *up* the Inclusion Dial without moving anyone else *down*. For example, as some organizational cultures have become more inclusive of women and nonbinary people, some men in those same cultures have become more afraid of the cost of inadvertently doing or saying the wrong things. We'll work to avoid these kinds of unintended effects by adhering to the principle that sustainable solutions to inclusion must make *everyone* better off.*

Finally, reflect on where you placed yourself on the Inclusion Dial. What would it take for *you* to move up? For the rest of the day, we'll be looking for both individual and collective opportunities for inclusion, but we'll give you the headline now: if we all take full responsibility for creating inclusive organizations and we all take full responsibility for sharing our uniqueness, then our chances of winning the inclusion sweepstakes are truly excellent.

> **GUT CHECK:** Proceed when you've collected data on the range of inclusion experiences in your organization—including your own.

---

*In our experience, this is not a difficult principle to preserve, in contrast with the high incidence of fixed-pie, us-or-them anxieties about DEI work.

Make It Physically and Emotionally
Safe to Be Different

If you're like most companies of a certain size (let's say a hundred or more employees), then a small percentage of your colleagues don't feel safe coming to work. If this pattern has been confirmed for you, either through the survey exercise we've proposed or by some other means, then we want to be clear: it's your human, moral, and institutional responsibility to take action. You have colleagues who may be in harm's way.

We're not saying that the way someone *feels* should be accepted as irrefutable truth (we've established our belief in the unreliability of perception). To feel unsafe on the job could mean many things. It could mean the absence of *psychological* safety—the focus of the next section—which is not the same thing as being in physical danger but is still bad news for the organization. It could be an indicator of a misunderstanding, or someone could be politicizing or even weaponizing the concept of safety, which we've seen happen more than once. But those are also real problems that need to be solved, and the bigger issue is that your teammates may in fact be experiencing an unacceptable level of risk when they come to work. The rest of this section assumes that a lack of safety is being reported in good faith. Indeed, while organizations must protect their people against the risk of false accusations, the prevalence of false reporting is low.[23] Meanwhile, 90 percent of people who say they have experienced harassment never take formal action such as filing a charge or a complaint.[24]

It's our obligation as leaders to reduce and prevent serious workplace harms through training, empowerment, and a culture of truth and consequences. We must also create systems where people can surface harms with as much grace and speed as possible. For example, we urge you to circle back to the group you surveyed anonymously and invite anyone feeling unsafe to give the organization a chance to address the problem. Offer a range of engagement options, not just HR (there's a reason they haven't used the existing systems to surface problems). Provide airtight assurances about privacy, retaliation, and other risks to speaking up.

Here's a way to think about this: As a foundation, you and your colleagues must feel physically and emotionally safe when you come to work. Period. You must feel like your chances of being harmed are reasonably low by the standards of your chosen profession.* For most people, in most jobs, this means you can go to work with the confidence that you're unlikely to be bullied, harassed, injured, or exposed to a serious health risk.** If you can't provide a baseline of security for your people, then don't bother focusing on the next three levels of the Inclusion Dial (or much else on your leadership agenda). You're unlikely to make progress.

Safety is rarely equitably denied, which is why we start our inclusion story here. When people ask us where to begin their DEI work, we advise them to protect and empower the people who are most likely to experience the absence of safety. For

---

*Meaning, simply, that the definition of reasonably low varies by field. For example, it differs for police officers versus high school teachers versus finance professionals.
**As we write this sentence, Buffalo Bills player Damar Hamlin is in the hospital fighting for his life after suffering acute injuries on the playing field, something that happens with grim regularity in American football. The NFL, which is in the *entertainment business*, is failing this test.

example, if your frontline teams are most likely to be harmed at the height of a viral pandemic, then they get to jump to the front of the inclusion line.

A common application of this principle is that you must confront the reality that female workers, people of color, and LGBTQ+ employees (particularly your trans colleagues) have a higher risk of being sexually harassed in the workplace than other demographics. Your colleagues who check two or more of those boxes are at the highest risk.[25] Organizations need clear-eyed strategies for preventing and addressing sexual misconduct that acknowledge these facts, reinforced by a culture that refuses to tolerate them.

How do you get this right? Involve the people most likely to be harmed in *co-producing* the strategies designed to serve them (recall Steinem's exasperated turtle from Tuesday). For example, the authors of this book walk around with a protective cloak of whiteness in America and have no idea what the fear of race-based violence or discrimination feels like. We shouldn't be working independently to reduce and respond to those harms, but that also doesn't mean we're off the hook. As our colleague Tina Opie challenges us in her own scholarship, it's our responsibility—and *opportunity*—to be great allies and partners to our teammates with different experiences of safety, and we must bring grace, humility, and urgency to the task.[26] Indeed, the higher up we find ourselves on the Inclusion Dial, the greater our imperative to reach down and help pull others up.

This tension showed up vividly for us when we began working with Uber on how the company could differentiate on safety. Midway through a discussion with company leaders on the principles that would inform such a strategy, we realized that half the room was talking about reducing the risks of harassment and violence—to both riders and drivers—in the intimate space of an enclosed vehicle. The other half was talking about reducing traffic accidents and insurance costs. Not surprisingly, gender explained much of the difference.

Neta Meidav, founder and CEO of Vault Platform, brought her own experience—and the experience she knew she shared with so many others—to the challenge of building safer workplaces. Fresh out of college, Meidav turned down her dream job after being harassed by the hiring manager. She chose not to report the incident: "I didn't trust the system to treat me fairly and was worried that my career would be crushed by a powerful man before it even started." Months later, Meidav found out the hiring manager had also harassed one of her peers: "If I had known this was a pattern, I would have come forward."

The software solution that Meidav and her team designed— a digital, app-based Speak Up platform that includes a feature called GoTogether—allows users to document incidents privately but wait to report them until there are other complaints about the same person. The option to take collective action removes a key barrier to reporting, while also letting employers know that there's someone on their payroll with a repeated pattern of harm. Vault's tools train users on what qualifies as a policy breach in their own organization and allows them to privately document and time-stamp things like inappropriate text messages. The company's technology makes it easier for people in harm's way to credibly fight back and hold their perpetrators accountable— progress made possible by Meidav's talent, courage, and willing- ness to bring her distinct perspective to the workplace.*

Disclosure: We were so impressed by the tools that Meidav and her team were devel- oping that we decided to advise and invest in the company.

Who or what is undermining safety in your own organization? One bad apple? The absence of robust HR systems (common in professional service firms and early-stage companies)? A culture of star performers that's getting in the way of taking action? By the way, the intuition behind star performer tension, to put it bluntly, is wrong. Toxic top performers may generate short-term wins, but their longer-term impact on performance is decidedly negative. While they may bring in more revenue, they also spur high churn of talented people and eventually erode a firm's culture and reputation.[27]

Finally, if *you're* not feeling safe, then put this book down and tell someone you trust about your experience. Break the silence that's propping up whatever or whomever is putting you at an unacceptable risk. With a trusted thought partner in your corner—and without the stress and pain of feeling radically alone—you'll be able to figure out the next right thing to do.

> **GUT CHECK:** Proceed when you have a plan to ensure the physical and emotional safety of everyone in your workplace.

Make It *Psychologically* Safe to Be Different

Some people reporting a lack of safety may not feel *psychologically* safe. Again, this is good news in that they're not at risk of imminent physical or emotional harm. But it's bad news in that they're encountering a serious barrier to their engagement, contribution, and performance. People who don't feel psychologically safe are

afraid to speak up—to share their ideas, questions, or concerns—
for fear of being rejected, embarrassed, or otherwise penalized.[28]

Remember that unique information that's so critical to performance? Your colleagues who don't feel psychologically safe are
essentially stockpiling it to protect themselves. They're concluding, correctly, that sharing the full extent of their knowledge is
too interpersonally risky. Psychological safety is typically created and destroyed at the team level, so whoever's reporting it as
an issue is unlikely to be alone in their frustration (a good place
to start in surfacing the problem is to find out what their boss is
up to).

How big a deal is psychological safety? We round it off to *huge*.
According to Amy Edmondson, the scholar who has done the
most to advance the world's understanding of the concept, psychological safety is foundational to the performance of teams
and organizations. For example, when Google spent *years* trying
to rigorously explain differences in performance across its own
highly skilled teams—a project they code-named "Aristotle"—
the company concluded that psychological safety explained
"everything."[29] More precisely, company leaders came to see it as
the "underpinning" for other key performance drivers, the thing
you need to have in place before other things—like having clear
goals and doing meaningful work—make any difference at all.[30]
Psychological safety, which Edmondson sometimes refers to as
interpersonal fearlessness, is the foundation on which the rest of
your company's hopes and dreams are built.

Your inclusion goals are no exception. Inclusion, too, requires
an underpinning of psychological safety.[31] And like physical and
emotional safety, it's rarely equitably distributed. For example,

men tend to experience higher psychological safety than women, and white employees tend to experience higher psychological safety than other groups.[32] Said differently, your colleagues who are bringing some kind of difference into the workplace are more likely to feel psychologically *unsafe*.

Modupe Akinola, professor of leadership and ethics at Columbia Business School, studies the intersection of stress and identity. According to Akinola, the "nature of being one of 'the only' makes an environment feel less psychologically safe."[33] The risk/reward calculus of speaking up can also be complicated by stereotypes. Akinola's research found that the decision to identify problems—and even the vocal tone used in the process—is a higher-stakes choice for Black women, who feel added pressure to avoid being perceived as conforming to an "angry Black woman" trope.

Although remote work has helped to improve some inclusion indicators, particularly those related to safety (we're less likely to be harmed in our own living rooms), it hasn't solved this issue. Catalyst, a nonprofit organization on a mission to "build workplaces that work for woman," found that 45 percent of female business leaders say it's difficult for women to speak up in virtual meetings.[34] We highlight this research because it speaks directly to the remedies—how to make sure *everyone* feels like they can use their voice, wherever groups are gathered—which in our framework is part of your safe-to-welcome challenge. (More to come on how to run a fantastically inclusive meeting, digital or otherwise.)

The point we're trying to make is this: like physical and emotional safety, psychological safety is foundational to any high-trust, high-speed organization. It's what poker players call *table stakes*. We bring it up at this point in the story because *the people least likely to feel psychologically safe are also the people least likely to feel included.* The rest of this chapter will help you solve this problem, but for more guidance on how to create psychological safety at the scale of an organization, we'll refer you happily to Edmondson's work (highlights include the importance of being open to feedback and building a "speak up" culture).[35] Many organizations—GitLab is one great example—have made Edmondson's research central to their own DEI efforts.[36] Edmondson is on a mission to illuminate the pathways (more like highways) between psychological safety, inclusion, and performance—and we're on a mission to maximize the number of people trying to keep up with her.

> **GUT CHECK:** Proceed when you're convinced of the importance of creating psychological safety for everyone in your workplace.

Welcome Everyone Despite Their Differences

Once you can confidently check all the safe boxes, you can get to work on your next challenge: making sure that everyone feels welcome in the workplace, including people who represent some kind of difference. That difference could be highly visible, such as Black and brown employees in a largely white environment, or it could be less visible, such as religion, political affiliation, or identifying as LGBTQ+. It could mean scraping together sick days and time for medical appointments for someone battling a "hidden" disability like MS. It could also mean being a single forty-something parent on a team populated by twenty-somethings with no problem attending frequent late-night meetings.

Colleagues who are underrepresented in some way should also feel as if they can bring an authentic version of themselves to the collective mission. They should feel as if they have the right to take up as much space as the people around them. This is where objectives such as fairness and equality often live in DEI work: *When I feel welcome, I know that I will get a fair and equal opportunity to contribute, achieve, and advance, despite the differences I may be bringing with me to work.*

Most organizations will find opportunities for welcome across the full HR life cycle (recruitment, development, promotion, and retention), and they will typically present as reducing bias and increasing belonging at each stage. For example, many US tech companies have successfully created workplaces where young, straight white men they know can thrive, but are having a much harder time recruiting, developing, promoting, and retaining women, people of color, LGBTQ+ people, people over the age of thirty-five, any intersectional combination therein, and the young, straight white men they *don't* know. (By "know," we mean people who are separated by one or two degrees and largely share the same networks, influences, and life experiences.)*

---

*Here's a simple, directional test: if the demographics of your team don't bear much resemblance to the demographics of the broader population, then you've likely put artificial barriers on the talent pools in which you're fishing, which means not only are you missing out on the rest of that beautiful pond of humanity, but you're also at risk of a culture of conformity.

What would a more welcoming HR life cycle look like, in tech and beyond? For one, it would mean doing things differently if you want a different outcome. For example, it would mean more actively recruiting in spaces where your out-groups—those identities that *aren't* thriving—are in the majority. This might mean skilled outreach to historically Black colleges and universities. And women's colleges. And colleges in geographies that are unfamiliar to you. For example, Duolingo, the breakthrough language-learning app, achieved a striking 50/50 gender ratio for new software engineers by making major changes to its recruiting strategy, including refusing to recruit at universities where fewer than 18 percent of women are represented in computer science programs (the national average).[37]

As you look for Tuesday-ish opportunities to *solve for trust* in your own HR life cycle, it might mean being more systematic about development opportunities. It might mean thinking harder about who gets staffed on high-visibility projects or who gets to join site visits with senior leaders. It might mean challenging squishy, subjective evaluation criteria such as "cultural fit," which live almost entirely in the eyes of overconfident beholders. It might mean changing the ways you assess people for promotion, which can be riddled with bias and pitfalls, particularly for women.[38]

When Kathleen Hogan, chief people officer at Microsoft, joined CEO Satya Nadella in executing one of the most exciting corporate turnarounds in a generation, she looked at every aspect of the employee experience through the lens of inclusion. Inclusion was one of Microsoft's three strategic can't-get-it-wrong priorities, and so Hogan made it an important part of performance evaluations. This meant, among other things, that impact on *others* would be measured alongside individual contribution, a radical shift for a tech company. By the time Hogan was done with her overhaul—and Microsoft's performance was spiking historically upward (remember all those links between inclusion and performance?)—individual impact still mattered to your advancement at the company, but just as important was how much you contributed to *other people's* success.[39]

Sometimes welcome can simply mean the absence of headwinds. One thing we like to do when we start working with companies is to sit down with senior people from underrepresented groups and ask, "What does this organization need to do to keep awesome people like you?" A straightforward answer we often get is to reduce the burden of a "representation tax" on their workload. Asking the same people to sit on hiring committees and be visible when stakeholders are in town, again and again, can backfire if it means they're doing significantly more uncredited work than their colleagues.

We're often asked for a summary of how to build a workplace where everyone feels welcome. Our short answer is to recruit great people you don't already know, give them interesting work to do, and invest in them as if your company's future depends on it. If they deserve a promotion, give it to them in a timely manner. Don't make them wait. Don't make them go to a competitor to get the role, title, and decision rights they already earned on your watch. And in the name of all that is right and just in the world, pay them fairly and equitably for the work they do.

In addition, chase down any uncomfortable demographic patterns in who's getting recruited, developed, promoted, and retained. Examine the root cause of any trends you find, which, like any problem (remember Monday?), may be more complex than it appears. As we've explored a few times in this book already, we are big believers in this type of tracking and analysis. What gets measured gets done, as the saying goes, and the accountability and transparency that these tools generate can be invaluable.

That said, DEI analytics must be thoughtfully timed and skillfully used. For example, they sometimes create unintended pressure to adopt blunt-force instruments such as diverse slates and hiring quotas, which can breed cynicism on all sides without creating the conditions for true inclusion. Like any approach, if tools like this are working for you, then keep using them. And if they're not, then stop.* Our own practical bias is to focus *most* of your energy on "supply side" opportunities at each stage of the HR life cycle, like more-inclusive recruiting, better training and mentoring, and more-equitable access to advancement opportunities. Demanding accountability for outcomes without giving the system a fighting chance to improve works about as well for companies as it does for people.

In most organizations, welcome is where DEI work begins and ends. That's not a bad thing, on its surface. To live in a world where everyone gets to feel safe and welcome when they go to work would be radical, beautiful progress. And yet the biggest gifts of inclusion—the point in your story where you gain an unbeatable advantage—occur higher up on the Inclusion Dial. In our view,

*Sometimes these tools are necessary to make progress toward a more equitable world when other strategies have failed. See histories of the civil rights movements in the United States and South Africa for the compelling case for mandates as a necessary but insufficient response to racial discrimination.

the reason to work so hard to get welcome right is that you get that much closer to *celebrated*, to a workplace where people are valued not *in spite of* our differences but *because of* our unique capacity to contribute. That's where we're headed next.

> **GUT CHECK:** Proceed when you understand the obstacles and accelerants to building an environment that welcomes difference.

Celebrate Uniqueness on Your Own Team

Once you can ensure that people feel safe and welcome, regardless of their differences, your next inclusion milestone is to make sure your teammates feel celebrated *because of* their uniqueness. To choose a perfectly random example, this is where a colleague might pivot in her experience from being a quirky, queer, forty-something woman with as good a chance as anyone else to contribute and advance—to being seen and valued for being *Anne.*

An organization that celebrates uniqueness assumes that difference is a source of creativity, innovation, and strength. It isn't just something to watch out for as it may get in the way of some people's contribution. When Tony Prophet was serving as chief equality and recruiting officer at Salesforce, he described the distinction this way: the real magic happens, he argued, when "you feel seen, you feel included, you feel *valued.*" That experience, in Prophet's view, becomes a competitive asset that's analogous to a mosaic, with distinct and complex pieces coming together to make a more magnificent whole: "The result is the beauty and the melding of ideas."[40]

Counterintuitively, *celebrated* is the point on the dial where we get to stop worrying so much about all those identity categories that we became appropriately focused on in the work of safe and welcome. We cared about identity as an organization lower on the dial because opportunity and harm were being inequitably distributed (or to put it more technically, because identity was an explanatory variable in the distribution of opportunity and harm). Said differently, we need to put people into categories when those categories are somehow still adversely impacting their experience of work.* You get to move on to celebrated when that's no longer true.

People tend to experience celebrated in the intimacy of teams, which is why you may have earned the numbers you did on your survey. If you were to look more closely at the responses, you'd likely find a clumping of celebrated around a few great managers. In the same way we pushed on your safe numbers, we urge you to circle back to the group you surveyed anonymously and invite anyone feeling high up on the Inclusion Dial to give the organization a chance to learn from their experience. Sample on these positive examples and look for patterns in who or what is contributing to people feeling seen, valued, and included in the organization. Turn the patterns you find into norms, policies, and expectations for organizational behavior.

We're confident that one pattern you will find among these superstar managers, the ones with whole teams that feel celebrated, is that they excel at the practice of setting high standards and revealing deep devotion simultaneously.** They're likely to be

---

*Here's our take on the right/left debate on DEI in America: the Right is arguing that we should be operating with the assumptions of Celebrated—namely, treating everyone as individuals—and the Left is arguing that we're not there yet; we still have a whole lot of Safe and Welcome work to do first.
**We explore this practice in depth in chapter 3 of *Unleashed*.

exceptional coaches, mentors, and *sponsors*, meaning that they're also advocating for their teammates when those teammates are not in the room.[41] They're also very likely to be creating a specific experience in meetings, one where contributing unique knowledge is valued and expected. We're going to pause here and get very tactical about what being on a team like this *feels* like.

As we asked you to do in our exploration of inclusion in *Unleashed*, imagine that you're a young Black or brown woman on a primarily white team. The meeting is scheduled, and you feel safe showing up. The guy who had been repeatedly asking you out via the company's Slack channel, despite you asking him to stop, has been removed from your team. You walk in and a white colleague makes you feel welcome by inviting you to sit next to her. The team lead—an older man—opens by saying, "I'd like to get your advice, and I want to hear from everyone." You're feeling pretty good at this point, comfortable and ready to participate.

The meeting continues, and there seems to be convergence in what the group thinks the plan should be. (Note that this is the point at which most organizations declare victory and move forward with an idea.) You have a different idea, but you don't want to rock the boat or hold the group back. Then the team lead says, "OK, if we were to think about this problem *differently*, what would that look like?" A few new voices jump into the discussion. The team lead says, "Great! I never would have thought of that. You're making our logic more rigorous."

He then says, "What else are we missing?" His response shifts the dynamics in the room, and you decide to share your idea. Your colleagues respectfully debate your idea; they identify some risks that you hadn't thought about before, but people seem energized by the ambition of it. The lead says, "Listen, it might not work, but I love the audacity of [insert your name]'s idea. It's the kind of thinking we need to win." You leave the meeting feeling valued by the company for your ability to think differently—and without any doubts that you belonged in the room.

This is what it looks like, in practice, to create workspaces where people reliably share their unique perspectives, experiences, and capabilities. In our work, we call that celebrated. May you be someone who is celebrated, may you lead a team where others are celebrated, too, and may you build an organization where celebrated is so embedded in the organization that it doesn't depend on the commitment and skill set of individual leaders like you. That's your next challenge.

> **GUT CHECK:** Proceed when you feel more confident in identifying and valuing the unique contributions of your colleagues.

Champion Uniqueness at the Scale of the Organization

The final frontier in building an inclusive organization is for the celebration of difference to become so ingrained institutionally that people feel championed for their uniqueness, with minimal variability across individuals, teams, and functions. This is the point of no return in your campaign for full belonging. It's the point at which we no longer feel "lucky" to have an inclusive manager, the point at which we're all taking exquisite care of people who are different from us with the unshakable confidence that their difference makes us better.

Another way to think about getting to championed is that you now get to focus on building a *culture* of inclusion.[42] For your celebrated-to-championed challenge, huddle with colleagues you trust—include those who feel the *least* included—and brainstorm Tuesday-like experiments in culture change that would help you foster greater inclusion. Assume best intentions: What must your smart, talented, gorgeous teammates need to *think* in order to *act* in a more inclusive way? How might you influence their thinking?

For Lars Fruergaard Jørgensen, president and CEO of the global pharmaceutical company Novo Nordisk, the answer was to cultivate shared conviction in the payoffs of inclusion: "I needed everybody on my management team to buy into . . . [the] belief that to succeed in our business, to adapt to a more diversified future . . . it's going to take different types of leadership, different types of market approaches, [openness] to new ways of working."[43]

But Jørgensen also discovered the importance of heading off *negative* beliefs about DEI work, particularly fears that some people would be left behind. "We're not down-prioritizing Danish men in light blue shirts," he found himself frequently clarifying, a reference to a light bulb moment Jørgensen experienced when he noticed that everyone onstage for a senior management meeting was a straight white Danish man over fifty wearing a light blue shirt, even as the company had growing ambitions to compete in an increasingly diverse number of global markets and demographic segments. "We are giving everyone the same opportunities, and that will create . . . more opportunities for all of us, compared to [perpetuating] a tunnel view and [missing] the diversity of the opportunity out there. . . . It's actually making all of us stronger."[44]

Ideas that have come out of some of the brainstorming sessions we've hosted on inclusion included job swaps (e.g., leaders spending a week on the front lines), improvements to hiring policies (e.g., ensuring that applicants get feedback, Mignon Early–style, on why they didn't get the job), and changes to advancement criteria (e.g., adding the demonstration of inclusive behaviors to requirements for leadership roles).

If I'm being sent to the front lines as a high-status leader, for example, then I'm more likely to conclude that the voices of frontline workers matter. If I'm being asked to spend time giving internal candidates real feedback on why they didn't get the job, then I'm more likely to view my job as developmental and not just evaluative. And if my advancement prospects depend on my ability to include others, then I'm more likely to dig in and figure out what this inclusion stuff is all about.* By the time you're finished making sure people feel championed, your Even Better Plan has a chance of becoming a Very Good Plan.

> **GUT CHECK:** Proceed when you're ready to champion authenticity at the scale of your organization.

---

*As we hope you internalized yesterday, if experiments like these succeed in fostering new ways of thinking, then scale them up; and if they don't, then try something else.

Include Yourself, Too

Most of us are not working in environments where we feel celebrated or championed today. If we had to summarize our own mission in doing the work we do, it's to make that statement obsolete. Said more hopefully, if not more poetically, we hope to do our part to help move as many people as possible up the Inclusion Dial. If we can create a world where more people can truly thrive in more workplaces, then our species gets to fix more of our problems faster.

There are both institutional and individual barriers to the arrival of that new world. In her novel *The Shipping News*, the great Annie Proulx observed, "We're all strange inside. We learn how to disguise our differences as we grow up."[45] We welcome Proulx's reminder that we have some agency over how much of ourselves we share with the world. If we're the ones disguising our differences, then we're also the ones with the power to unmask them, which means we don't have to wait to be ourselves until the world figures out how to crack the code on inclusion.

How do we include *ourselves*, too? How and *when* do we risk authenticity in imperfect conditions? To be our "real selves" sounds nice in theory, but there can be powerful, hard-earned incentives to hold back certain truths. No one comes by Proulx's disguises casually. The decision to cover up our differences can be highly practical, if wrenching, as in the decision to stay closeted in a workplace that's hostile to queer identities or to continuously police our words to avoid harmful stereotypes.

Believe us when we say we know this is hard—and sometimes too much to ask. At every step of our careers, we've been tempted to dilute who we are in the world. Although we're as white as they come, we're also unambiguously queer women with strongly held opinions and overt ambition, for ourselves and others. One of us holds her breath in public bathrooms, knowing that she's likely to be misgendered. In most of the workplaces we enter, these things make us different.

But as we've written about before, if those of us who are different give in to the pressure to hold back our authentic selves, then we suppress the most valuable parts of ourselves. Not only do we end up concealing the very thing the world needs most from us— our uniqueness—but we also make it harder for people to trust us in leadership, continuing a cycle of diminishment that keeps the status quo firmly in place. The smaller we choose to make ourselves, the less likely we are to take up the space required to lead.

Taking up leadership space requires intention, we've learned, and a willingness to challenge our own primal stories.[46] The part of your brain that's wired for survival does an excellent job of protecting you, but it shouldn't always be calling the shots. For one thing, it's not playing the long game. The stories it's telling you ("What other people think of you is very important!") are designed to get you to the end of the day, not to the end of a life filled with meaning and impact.

One way to calm this part of your brain is to discover your own authenticity hacks (or *boosters*, if you prefer). Figure out what tends to draw your complex humanity back up to the surface. Your beloved nephew? Favorite sports team? Passion for Wonder

Woman trivia? Surround yourself with reminders of these things or—better yet—find ways to somehow bring them with you into spaces where an inauthentic version of you has a habit of showing up. Frances peppers her Zoom background with pictures of our family. Anne likes to put a few of our son's Lego pieces in her pocket during big presentations.

Our most urgent advice is to build a Team (capital T) of friends and colleagues around you who can help you stay connected to the real you. Make it a requirement of Team membership that everyone is as comfortable with your insecurity as your audacity. Spend time with your Team on a very regular basis, no less than monthly.[47]

We've given you hints to the punch line throughout this chapter, and we'll spell it out for you here: if we all take full responsibility for building inclusive organizations, and we all take full responsibility for showing up in them authentically, then we dramatically improve our chances of Accelerating Excellence. In other words, we get to crush that Inclusion Dial.

> **GUT CHECK:** Proceed when you're committed to making new friends.

THURSDAY

Tell a Good Story

D epending on how you measure it, up to 70 percent of organizational change efforts fail.* We'll repeat ourselves, once more with feeling, since it's such a sobering truth: *more than half* of the talented, well-intentioned people who attempt to do what you're doing end up experiencing some version of defeat.

We're sharing this statistic with you because we believe you now have what you need to begin defying these odds in the building blocks of your Very Good Plan. You know the problem you're going to solve and you have a working, evidence-based plan for the solution. You've also made sure that *everyone* you're going to need feels safe, welcome, celebrated, and championed. These are the baseline requirements for activating the organization,

---

*While there's some healthy academic debate about the precision of this number, the reason this statistic is so resonant in our work is that it lines up with most people's experience. Changing organizations is hard—and more often than not, it doesn't work.

which is what you're going to begin doing today. We often refer to Thursday as "Storytelling Day."

Today's mission is to tell a story so powerful, so clear and compelling, that it will unleash your company's energy and channel it in the direction of change. You're going to build on the good work you've done earlier in the week and explain not only *why* the organization needs to change but also *how* it will change, what the future will look like in vivid and specific terms.

Today you will be *using your words*. Your words have the power to change the organization by shaping the attitudes and beliefs of the people inside it, starting with you. The story you tell yourself, the story in which you choose to live (and often more important, choose *not* to live), will set the terms and conditions of your new reality. And when you skillfully tell that story to other stakeholders, you begin to scale your new reality to the size of the company.

Howard Gardner, the great developmental psychologist, put it this way: "Stories constitute the single most powerful weapon in a leader's arsenal."[1] Today you'll use that weapon to break the rhetorical bonds keeping you trapped in Reckless Disruption or Responsible Stewardship or any other part of the landscape you no longer want to occupy. You'll liberate yourself and your colleagues to become the team you're earning the right to be this week. To do all of that, you'll need a good story.

Understand Deeply to Describe Simply

In our childhood homes, there was a short list of approved discussion topics: the weather, the pets, and Tom Brokaw, for some

THURSDAY'S AGENDA

1. Understand deeply to describe simply.

2. Honor the past (the good stuff).

3. Honor the past (the not-so-good stuff).

4. Provide a clear and compelling change mandate.

5. Describe a rigorous and optimistic way forward.

6. Put the pieces of your story together.

7. Repeat yourself.

8. Identify and use your emotions.

Materials You'll Need for Today

- Creativity

- Poster board or other medium for public writing

- Clear-eyed understanding of the organization's history, both the good stuff and the not-so-good

- Tolerance for repetitive tasks such as telling the same story again and again

- Access to someone with deep institutional memory and (preferred) high attachment to the "way things are"

- A poem you like or, at minimum, don't hate (if you don't know where to go with this one, just pick anything by Mary Oliver)

---

reason.* It was understood that words should be approached with caution. In retrospect, it's no surprise that we both ended

*Our siblings may recall things differently, but let's find out if they ever read this far into the book.

up talking and writing for a living, learning how to handle this controlled substance with care.

After a few decades of being in conversation with the world, our primary observation is this: the foundation of persuasive communication—communication that will change the way people think and act—is to understand something so *deeply* that you can describe it *simply*. If you understand something deeply but can only describe it in a complex or jargony way, then you only get to talk to the subset of people who speak your esoteric language. If you understand something only superficially, then your words will not survive out in the wild, where the pressure to dismiss them is relentless, even if you're the boss.

The objective of change storytelling is to understand the story deeply enough that you can describe it simply to the people you want to act on that story. One of our favorite examples of a deeply/simply change narrative is the one that fueled T-Mobile's resurrection from a company teetering on the edge of irrelevance to a serious industry player. T-Mobile understood its story at such a deep level that it figured out how to communicate it in a single word: *un-carrier.*

Instead of trapping customers into confusing service plans and then pummeling them with hidden fees (industry-standard, please-hate-us behaviors), T-Mobile offered low rates, clear plans, and transparent fees, working to become everything the wireless industry wasn't, to feel everything the rest of the industry didn't. It became the *un-carrier.*

The turnaround strategy itself wasn't simple—there were lots of moving parts—but T-Mobile understood it at a cellular level. Jon Legere, the company's swaggering CEO at the time, described it this way: "Un-carrier was an attitude and a culture and a behavior. . . . It was about finding and solving customer pain points in an attempt to fix a stupid, broken, arrogant industry."[2]

While the entire sector seemed to go out of its way to destroy consumer trust, Legere and his team built it up quickly by doubling down on all three trust drivers. There was clear *logic* to pursuing a pro-consumer opening on the strategic chessboard, and the company's product innovations revealed genuine *empathy* for what the industry was putting us all through. T-Mobile also walked the talk with an *authenticity* that consumers embraced. Its new, on-your-side values informed everything from the accessible language in its "Un-carrier Manifesto" to the wardrobe choices of Legere himself, who paired suits with bright T-shirts and sneakers, a departure for corporate CEOs at the time.

T-Mobile even made up the word *un-carrier*, underscoring the boldness of the company's vision. It's Lewis Carroll–grade audacity, which brings us to that poem on your packing list today.* Now is a good time to dust it off and read it aloud (poetry should be heard). Go further and consider hosting a reading with some of your fellow storytellers in the company. Ask everyone to share language that has moved them. Listen for how different words sound when they're whisked and stirred with intention.

What do you want to say to your colleagues about the world you want to build together? Can you capture it in a page? A paragraph? *A single word?* Mark Twain once apologized for writing a long letter, explaining that he didn't have time to write a short

---

*In his epic poem "Jabberwocky," Carroll blended English with a completely invented language that gave us words like *chortle* and *galumphing* and *frumious* (a personal favorite), a combination of *fuming* and *furious*.

one. Write your stakeholders the equivalent of a short letter—which, it turns out, may take you some extra time.

> **GUT CHECK:** Proceed when you deeply understand the change story you want to tell.

Honor the Past (the Good Stuff)

Let's break your story into distinct parts, at least for now. We suggest you start by looking backward, although it may seem counterintuitive (change is about the future, right?). Start by honoring the company's history and reflecting on all the things you *don't* want to change. The reality is that no one's getting onboard your change train unless you can convince us that you get it, that you truly understand the organization, starting with all the good stuff.

Here's a practical way to look at it: There will always be self-appointed gatekeepers who are resistant to change. Always, always, always. These are typically good people who have long institutional memories, care deeply about the organization, and worry most about what may be lost in all the flux and churn you're proposing. To bring these gatekeepers along—and reassure the parts within all of us (hi, again, Uncle Dick!) who dislike uncertainty—make it clear that you will preserve what's best about the company.

Change may make a whole lot of logical sense, but it can also be unsettling and disruptive to the people impacted by it. There are likely to be individual winners and losers along the way.

Reveal that you understand this anxiety. You may not share it, but you *get* it. In fact, we suggest keeping at least one gatekeeper close to you this week so that you experience that anxiety up close. You're more likely to honor it if it's something you can see and feel.

In one study of organizations embarking on large-scale change initiatives, a key finding was that employees feared the company would no longer be the company they valued and identified with—and the higher the uncertainty surrounding the change, the more employees worried about losing the organizational identity they cherished.[3] These researchers found that leaders were more effective in building support for change when they also emphasized continuity.

It's easy to become so focused on the things you want to change that you miss the opportunity to communicate what you genuinely *don't* want to change. This is a self-inflicted wound that's highly avoidable because there's always something about the organization you want to keep. You wouldn't be doing this work otherwise.

When Dara Khosroshahi hosted his first town hall meeting as Uber's new CEO, it would have been tempting to highlight the company's very public missteps and set himself up as Uber's savior. Instead, he committed to "retain the edge that made Uber a force of nature," which was met with thunderous employee applause. He also joined in a standing ovation for the company's former CEO, Travis Kalanick.

We were struck by Khosroshahi's grace in this moment, and that's the word we want you to channel. Have some grace for the people around you who aren't so sure about all your big plans, the skeptics and the resisters, and the simply scared. Make room for those people in your heart—and in your story—which means honoring the past they may be holding on to tightly.

> **GUT CHECK:** Proceed when you know what you
> want to preserve about the organization.

Honor the Past (the Not-So-Good Stuff)

As we've been exploring all week, we'll remind you that if your company has "wobbled" on trust with a particular set of stakeholders, then you need to rebuild that trust before earning the right to push forward. For example, spurred by Susan Fowler's courageous blog post, Khosroshahi combined his commitment to retain what was best about Uber with a pledge to do deep culture change work.*

This work must inform your storytelling, too. Many efforts to build greater inclusion, like Uber's, require a public reckoning with an organization's past. In January 2014, Dean Nitin Nohria apologized for Harvard Business School's historical treatment of women in extraordinary remarks that acknowledged that HBS women had felt "disrespected, left out, and unloved by the school." "The school owed you better," he declared unequivocally, "and I promise it will be better."[4]

---

*In February 2017, after leaving Uber, Fowler blogged about her experience of harassment and discrimination in a culture she convincingly portrayed as ruthless. Her post resonated broadly with female tech workers and sparked a backlash against sexual harassment in Silicon Valley.

His words rocketed around alumnae networks and meant a lot to us personally. When people ask us how an organization can heal from a painful past, we often reflect on Nohria's grace-filled example. In our experience, many leaders need to confront their organization's history with both optimism and honesty. Optimism is about building a better tomorrow, fixing an organization's problems with the kind of humility and ambition we explore throughout this book. Honesty is about taking radical responsibility for the things that went wrong and the human costs of those mistakes.

Riot Games made this choice when it responded to very public allegations of a fractured, sexist culture. A few days after the allegations surfaced, the company issued a clear-eyed apology it posted on its website. "To all those we've let down," the apology began, "we're sorry. We're sorry that Riot hasn't always been—or wasn't—the place we promised you. And we're sorry it took so long for us to hear you."[5] We find ourselves referencing this letter frequently in our work as an example of how to take clear, unequivocal responsibility for a painful past.

Riot's plainspoken apology runs counter to the instincts of many companies who are called out for historic missteps. When data engineer Frances Haugen challenged Meta to work harder to protect its most vulnerable users, the company's first response was to try to undermine her credibility as a messenger (good luck with that) rather than acknowledge the harms she rigorously documented.[6] Haugen won the round, in our view, sparking a tide of public frustration with the company, a drop in its stock price, and an increase in regulatory scrutiny.[7] Notably, Haugen wasn't taking a scorched-earth, burn-it-all-down approach: she invited Meta to move fast and fix things, an invitation the company seemed to decline. Riot, in contrast, said yes.

You don't need to have all the answers to begin this process. You do need to be willing to look unflinchingly at your history and begin the work of dealing with it. When Riot closed its letter with a pledge to "make Riot a place we can all be proud of" in the weeks, months, and years to come, the company didn't have every detail of the plan worked out. What it did know was that it needed a plan.

> **GUT CHECK:** Proceed when you're willing to confront the harms the organization has caused (and may still be causing).

Provide a Clear and Compelling Change Mandate

Now that you've opened your audience's heart to your message, even slightly, it's time to give the people what they want: a clear and compelling reason for *why* the organization needs to change. This part of your story is the second part of the three-part narrative you're building. You've honored the past—the good, bad, and ugly—and now you're going to give us a powerful rationale for creating a different future.

As a starting place, reflect back on the diagnostic work you did on Monday. What problem did you find? How does that problem pose a threat to the organization? Your answers must spur enough organizational action to move quadrants on that FIX map and override the comfort of familiar attitudes and behaviors. Among the challenges you will encounter on that expedition is Kanter's Law, which posits that *everything looks like a failure in the middle*.[8] Your fellow adventurers will need good reasons to press on, which is what you're now articulating.

When CEO Patrick Doyle launched a turnaround of Domino's, in response to slumping sales and an underwhelming stock price, he needed to break through the malaise that had settled into the company's corporate structure. Domino's was among the biggest food brands on the planet, having delivered (literally) on its radical promise to hand you a pizza in record time. The problem? As one reporter pointed out at the time, "You then had to eat it." In fact, consumers had decided that Domino's pizza tasted so bad that they liked it *less* when they found out who made it.[9]

Doyle and his team—led by CMO Russell Weiner (who has since been elevated to CEO*)—decided to shock the system by shining a big, bright spotlight on customers' frustration. They tracked scathing customer feedback and then shared it in national ads and on a giant, uncensored digital billboard in Times Square in New York City. Real-time comments such as "worst excuse for pizza I've ever had" and "tastes like cardboard" scrolled in massive letters in the most visible town square in America.

The predictable move would have been for the team to stay in Responsible Stewardship and quietly chip away at the problem, downplaying and rationalizing the market's negative reviews. Instead, they created the fuel to Accelerating Excellence by making

---

*We should disclose that moving fast and fixing things has a number of side effects, including higher rates of promotion.

the reason to change vividly clear to their stakeholders. There was now no escaping that Domino's had a problem or that the company was willing to take full responsibility for it. According to Weiner, "By saying what we said about the pizza, we blew up the bridge. That's what made it so much more powerful. If it didn't work out, there was no place to retreat to. There was no going back."[10, 11]

Domino's spurred action by telling everyone it could find about its terrible-tasting pizza, including customers (the effort was dubbed "Pizza Turnaround," which hit the right deeply/simply notes). By leveling with consumers instead of trying to spin them, the company sent a powerful authenticity signal. It also got the market very directly engaged by elevating its feedback (literally) to billboard-quality copy. Customers were given an essential, truth-telling role in the campaign—and an excellent reason to pay attention to what happened next. No longer on the sidelines, waiting for Domino's to do all the work, customers were helping to *co-produce* the fix.*

What happened next ended up being good for everyone. Domino's pizza got a whole lot better, and the market responded quickly and positively. Pizza Turnaround generated same-store sales growth of more than 10 percent in less than a year, and the company's stock price took off.

> **GUT CHECK:** Proceed when you can describe
> why the organization needs to change
> in clear, compelling language.

---

*This is a good example of a growing trend of customers playing any number of operating roles previously reserved for paid employees. As you think about your own operating plan, don't rule out your customers as potential participants in the value-creation process.

Describe a Rigorous and Optimistic Way Forward

And now for part three of your change narrative: a description of *how* the organization is going to change. This is the big reveal, the part where the tension gets resolved and we learn about your Very Good Plan for solving the organization's problem. Use the good work you did on Tuesday and Wednesday to motivate this part of the story. What did you learn that revealed the path forward? What convinced you that the direction you're championing is the right one? How confident are you that the road is truly passable?

As you work out your answers, you want to send two important signals: rigor and optimism. For the rigor part, use this as an opportunity to reinforce the *logic* pillar of your organizational trust triangle. Tell us all about your change strategy and operating plan to deliver on it. Note that those of you in Reckless Disruption may be tempted to skip over this part and simply ask your stakeholders to trust you. In short, they won't, not the ones you want to stick around: your strongest board members and best employees. Appeal to their own logic by revealing the depth of yours.

Data is your friend here, so get comfortable with the numbers. Take a good look at all of them, and then pick a *few* to use as plot points in the story. Less is more when it comes to data and storytelling. When the Danish company Ørsted reinvented itself in record time from a graying, old-school power company to one of the planet's leading providers of renewable energy—an extraordinary transformation—management focused the team on a single ratio: 85 percent. Instead of generating 85 percent of its energy from fossil fuels, a mix that had defined the business for decades, the company would flip that number on its head. In the not-so-distant future, 85 percent of Ørsted's energy would originate from sustainable sources such as wind and solar.[12]

The team labeled the turnaround plan "85/15," and it addressed the hard truths of the company's strategic exposures (climate change, inevitable depletion of fossil fuel stores) with boldness and, yes, rigor. Former CEO Henrik Poulsen credits the rigor part with bringing along an initially skeptical workforce: "We set a long-term vision, then translated it into a strategic business ambition with tangible targets to guide it. Then we rolled that back into action items for each employee to focus on over the next year."[13] Given the ambition of 85/15, Ørsted had targeted a turnaround goal of one generation, the equivalent of thirty years. The company ended up hitting its target in nine, *twenty-one years ahead of schedule.*

Now for the optimism part. If you've made it to Thursday, then you believe in the company's future, so please give your stakeholders unrestricted access to that conviction. Jeff Bezos famously asks his team to make the rigorous case for new ideas in very structured, six-page memos. He less famously asks them to pair those memos with imaginary press releases, in part, to test for the presence of genuine enthusiasm.[14] Regardless of where you sit in the organization, an important part of your job right now is to be the chief change evangelist (CCE), a self-appointed position with only one key responsibility: recruit converts to the vision. Optimism is a highly infectious emotion that is among your most effective conversion tools.

Just 15 percent of US employees strongly agree that their organization's leadership makes them feel enthusiastic about the future.[15] In our experience, this astonishing statistic is an unforced error with a relatively simple fix: tell us about your rigorous and optimistic way forward.

> **GUT CHECK:** Proceed when you can describe your plan for change in a way that inspires confidence.

Put the Pieces of Your Story Together

The research is overwhelming that stories are the best way to teach, inspire, and connect with our fellow human beings. We use stories to make sense of the world and our place in it. As anthropologist Mary Catherine Bateson once concluded, "The human species thinks in metaphors and learns through stories."[16] You've got enough on your plate without also trying to fight biology, so let's go tell a good story.

Ursula Burns, as CEO of Xerox, led the company out of its competitive wilderness by making a massive pivot from manufacturing to services. Stories were the currency of Burns's transformative tenure: "One of the things I learned," she reflected, "was that stories matter, communications matter, putting things in context matters."[17] Burns spent countless hours meeting with stakeholders from around the world and making it clear that massive change was the only way forward—and that there was a better Xerox on the other side of it: "Telling people the reality of what's going on and giving them hope by providing them with the vision and idea for what it's going to look like when we get through this is fundamental. It's foundational to having people follow you."[18]

Take Burns's lead and put your own change story together in a way that honors the past, articulates the change mandate, and provides a rigorous and optimistic vision for the future. Start by literally writing out the story in a simple, three-part structure using the following chapter headings: "The Good Ol' Days," "The Change Mandate," and "The Optimistic Way Forward."* Your story may not fit cleanly into this architecture, but we're going to challenge you to try it our way first. We promise that something useful will come out of the exercise.

If it's practical, do the exercise with a team (it's a nice follow-on to your poetry reading) and then share what you've written beyond the group to test and improve the story. As always, don't rule out your customers as potential resources here. Ask trusted customers for feedback—or take inspiration from Domino's and give them their own direct voice in the story. A shift in market dynamics is often a powerful change motivator, and your customers may be the best messengers of that shift.

You also don't have to limit yourself to words (and the occasional number). When Jan Carlzon led the turnaround of Scandinavian Airlines (SAS)—still among the most successful turnarounds in business history—he circulated a small, illustrated, comic-style book that used a cartoon plane to describe

---

*By the way, if "The Good Ol' Days" weren't all that good, we're still going to push you to honor what the organization got right. No one reading *this* book is planning to burn it all down, so there must be something that's worth recognizing and preserving. If the good stuff was limited or left some people behind, put that part of the story in the "The Change Mandate."

FIGURE 4-1

The SAS plane is sad

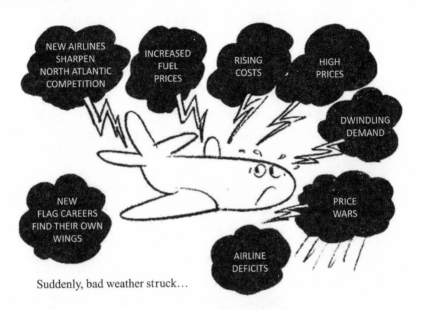

Suddenly, bad weather struck...

Source: Jan Carlzon, *Let's get in there and fight!* (Scandinavian Airlines System, 1981), https://www
.slideshare.net/karina_nik/lets-get-in-there-and-fight-by-jan-carlzon-sas-eng-only.

the company's pivot to a market-oriented strategy anchored in delighting business travelers. Figure 4-1 excerpts one of our favorite pages from this book, which captured Carlzon's change mandate in a single image featuring one sad plane and a few scattered words.

Carlzon's senior colleagues were convinced that SAS's highbrow, cerebral Scandinavian workforce would reject the form—instead, the opposite happened. The book was embraced as a clear North Star to help the company navigate its own choppy change waters.[19]

If you question the relevance of books in the age of digital communications, we'll refer you to Marguerite Zabar Mariscal, visionary, thirtysomething CEO of Momofuku, a cutting-edge restaurant and retail brand that continued to thrive in the chaos of the Covid-19 pandemic.[20] Mariscal commissioned beautifully designed, pocket-size "guidebooks" once the company reached one thousand employees, the scale at which she could no longer rely on intimate storytelling to capture the company's past, present, and future. Every new employee, from dishwashers to sous-chefs to the head of operations, gets a copy of the guidebook.[21]

Use words, cartoons, pictures, numbers—any means necessary—to bring your change story to life. Don't be afraid to invite your inner eight-year-old to the exercise. Make the process tactile and fun and stay open to the unexpected. When we walked a large, multinational firm through this exercise, the senior team broke through a strategic logjam that had been in place for years. One participant exclaimed, "We saved three years in thirty minutes!" We're going to be generous here and give you the full day to try it on your own.

> **GUT CHECK:** Proceed when you can tell a compelling story about the organization's past, present, and future.

Repeat Yourself

Now tell your story everywhere you find yourself talking: speeches, interviews, town hall meetings, team huddles, one-to-one conversations. You can play to your strengths as a storyteller, but don't stop there. Push yourself outside your comfort zone and experiment with different formats and media. For example, high-quality, well-edited video is now easy to make and remains a strangely underutilized change-leadership tool (even as we watch TikTok take off at remarkable speed). Pop up on the portable movie screen in every one of your employees' pockets and show-not-tell us a great change story.

Here's our headline for this part of your agenda: change leaders need to communicate far more often than they think is necessary. Some guidance we're confident in giving you is that whatever you're doing, it's not enough. In our experience, you likely need to up the frequency of your strategic communication by two to three times.

You have other important things to do, so why go to all the trouble? Frequent communication calms down our anxious parts and ensures that busy, distracted humans understand the story—understand it to the point where it can reliably inform their *own* actions. This is a core objective of change leadership: to set other people up to succeed in your *absence*. As we'll explore in more detail tomorrow, absence leadership is essential to organizational speed, as it removes you as a bottleneck to progress and empowers other people to sprint without your oversight. Repetition, it turns out, is foundational to empowerment.

Former Ford CEO Alan Mulally talked incessantly about his "One Ford" turnaround plan. He started *every meeting* he convened by reviewing the plan and distributed it on wallet-size cards to every Ford employee. Bryce Hoffman, author of a book on Mulally's run at Ford, said, "After six months, those of us who followed the company had gotten sick of hearing about [it]." When Hoffman asked Mulally about sharing "something new" in an interview, Mulally looked at him like he was crazy. "But, Bryce," he replied incredulously, "we're still working on this plan. Until we achieve these goals, why would we need another one?"[22] Mulally's relentlessness paid off. In less than four years, he pulled Ford back from the brink of bankruptcy and led the company to become one of the most profitable automakers in the world.

A research team led by our colleagues Tsedal Neeley and Paul Leonardi validated Mulally's instincts. After shadowing leaders in six companies for more than 250 hours, recording every communication the leaders sent and received, they discovered that the leaders who were deliberately redundant moved their projects forward faster and more smoothly. Reflecting on the research, Leonardi noted: "We're so bred to believe that clarity is the key to being a better communicator. . . . it's [actually] about making your presence felt. Employees are getting pulled in many directions and reporting to lots of people and getting tons of communications. So how do you keep your issues top of mind? Redundancy is a way to do that."[23]

HubSpot founder Dharmesh Shah put it this way: "It took me 20+ years as an entrepreneur to start to recognize the power of repetition—and even then it's still uncomfortable for me." But discomfort, Shah argues, is a reliable signal that you're on the right track. He continued: "It's natural for it to feel unnatural. Unnatural, but profoundly necessary."[24] One measure of your success today: Are you sick of hearing yourself talk?

> **GUT CHECK:** Proceed when you're tired of hearing yourself tell your change story.

Identify and Use Your Emotions

We're going to end the day talking about emotion, an underexplored or at least under *discussed* part of change leadership. (For a summary of our favorite public emotions, see "Ten Underrated Emotions in the Workplace.") Evolution has taught us to pay careful attention to one another's emotions, particularly the emotions of people with power over us. This kind of unconscious, somatic vigilance can be both an asset and a liability for leaders. As we've discussed, it means that optimism is highly infectious—but so is anxiety, for example.

Convinced that gratitude was worth unleashing in the workplace, legendary PepsiCo CEO Indra Nooyi made a habit of sending thank-you notes to the *parents* of her senior team, thanking them for sharing the gift of their child with PepsiCo. She wrote more than four hundred letters a year, with extraordinary results. Pause and imagine the effect of a practice like that in your own company: How would people feel about showing up to contribute? Some of Nooyi's executives—all highly accomplished—reported that it was the *best thing that had ever happened to them.*[25]

Daniel Goleman, who developed the idea of emotional intelligence, would call Nooyi's letters an example of *primal leadership.* He described the phenomenon this way: "The leader's mood is quite literally contagious, spreading quickly and inexorably throughout the business. . . . The same holds true in the office, boardroom, or shop floor; group members inevitably "catch" feelings from one another."[26] When you step up to leadership, whether you like it or not, there's no option to turn off the broadcast feature on whatever you're feeling.

Organizations got a lot of practice with this one in the early days of the recent pandemic. A research team at Harvard sought to decipher the communications lessons from this moment in crisis leadership, sending an assessment to more than one thousand employees in organizations that were disrupted by the virus. One key finding was that the emotional note leaders hit was a major variable in the experience of their employees. It was so important, in fact, that it could make or break an employee's commitment to the company. One respondent reported, "[Our leader's] calls with us and reassurances that the company has our back are inspiring. I even used it as a humble brag on social media to make sure people know we are still hiring and that this is the sort of company you want to work for when the going gets tough."[27]

Self-awareness is the key to skillfully playing the "instrument" of your emotions and preventing your feelings from sabotaging your change story. Accepting your emotions, integrating them into your actions, is also an opportunity to build trust and reinforce authenticity. The opposite—trying to suppress or deny what you're feeling (what, me vulnerable?)—is an inauthenticity tell that's easy to read. To help you get there and make peace with what you're feeling, below are ten emotions that deserve more respect at work.

Counterintuitively, emotional mastery can sometimes look to the outside world like doing nothing at all. We're going to set a high bar for this one, which is to take leadership lessons from Abraham Lincoln. As our colleague Nancy Koehn explores in her fascinating study of crisis leadership, Lincoln was able to resist taking immediate action, even in the face of extraordinary pressure to do something, *anything* in response to apparent disaster. Koehn writes, "In our own white-hot moment, when so much

Ten Underrated Emotions in the Workplace

We believe that emotions, generally, are underrated at the office. If you're a woman of a certain age, as we are, then you may have been cautioned against letting something as messy as a *feeling* accompany you to work. And if you're a man of a certain age, as we're sometimes mistaken for (wink), then you may have been rewarded for what appeared to be the absence of emotion.[28] These messages have conspired to create a missed opportunity. In addition to being powerful tools of persuasion and influence, emotions ground us in our humanity—useful when we're around other humans—and give us important data about our environments. The trick, of course, is to notice our feelings and put them to work without letting them hijack our brain's control system. To help illustrate this point, below are some of our favorite emotions that are undervalued in the workplace. Not all of them are technically emotions, but you get the idea:

1. **Frustration.** Next-level, serial entrepreneur Paul English has tapped into frustration for every one of his breakthrough ideas, including channeling it into the launch of metasearch engine Kayak after he couldn't believe how much time he was spending going from one airline website to another to try to find the best flight.[29] When English guest lectures to MBA students, he challenges them to come to class with a picture of something that annoys them. More often than not, a legitimate idea for a business is born at some point in the class.

2. **Regret.** A variation on frustration, regret typically shows up at the boundary of self and other. We regret a careless comment we made to a colleague, for example, or

(continued)

we regret not saying The Thing at the moment The Thing would have made a difference. As uncomfortable as it is to sit with regret, it often shows us what to do differently next time. It may also give us clues to what we may need to clean up. If you're still regretting that comment three days later, it's a pretty good signal that you may need to apologize.

3. **Enthusiasm.** This may surprise our global readers, but even Americans are cautioned against being too enthusiastic at work. In fact, one of us was once advised never to use the word *excited* as a woman, with its suggestion of an unruly, downright *feminine* lack of control. Call it something else if you want, but don't forget that the most effective change leaders are evangelical about the world they're building and reveal their enthusiasm at every turn.

4. **Devotion.** Humans thrive in a context of high standards and deep devotion, defined as full-bodied, unapologetic commitment to someone else's success. We sometimes hold back the full extent of our devotion based on the false belief that it will somehow get in the way of the high standards part. In short, it won't, so please make it very clear how much you want your colleagues to crush it.*

5. **Happiness.** Tony Hsieh, may he rest in deep peace, showed us all the power of sparking joy at work, building his shoe empire Zappos on a foundation of happy employees, customers, and suppliers. And yet. We're still making each other miserable in the workplace at rates that are far too high. Let Hsieh's legacy be that we listen more closely to what he came here to tell us.

6. **Discomfort.** This is one that we all get wrong, at least some of the time, by conflating discomfort with a signal to stop doing what we're doing. We're wired to avoid it as human beings, and yet so much of the good stuff happens outside our comfort zone, from learning something new to confronting a problem that we don't yet know how to solve. Take it from Virginia "Ginni" Rometty, former chairperson, president, and CEO of IBM: "Growth and comfort do not coexist."[30]

7. **Anger.** Yes, we think there's a place for anger, too, if for no other reason than suppressing anger will eventually convert it into an internal toxin. Anger is tricky on a bunch of levels, including the truth that we don't all get equal access to it. For example, Black professionals expressing anger at work are more likely to pay a price for that choice.[31] Anger is often a secondary emotion, a mask for more complicated feelings such as disappointment or sadness. When we coach people through this one, that's often the place we'll start. What might be living underneath the anger? What can you learn from *that* emotion?

8. **Joy.** Joy is one of legendary NBA coach Steve Kerr's four core team values (along with mindfulness, compassion, and competition), which he credits with fueling the Golden State Warriors' extraordinary success. The joy part often surprises people, at least until they see Kerr's Warriors cheerfully dominate the court.[32] By the way, joy is also not equitably accessed, which is why it's still an "act of resistance" for some of us.**

9. **Fellowship.** There's not a perfect word for what we mean here, so we'll simply put it this way: life brings all of us to

(*continued*)

our knees at some point. We need other people to help us get back up, in big and small ways. Chances are good that you'll meet some of those people at work.

10. **Grace.** This is the big one, we believe—the one that's far too scarce for the moment in which we're living and working. In our experience, grace starts as an inside job, meaning that we need to make space for our own flawed humanity before we can open up that circle to other people. Depending on your circumstances, grace might present as kindness, compassion, or generosity of spirit. It might be a decision to have the difficult conversation or to *not* have the difficult conversation. However it shows up, grace demands that we practice on ourselves before we're credible conduits to others.

*For a longer discussion of the mechanics of setting high standards and revealing deep devotion, see chapter 3 of *Unleashed*, which we titled "Love." We believe that creating the conditions for someone else to thrive and evolve is among the purest forms of love.

**The breathtaking line "Joy is an act of resistance" first appears as a revolutionary call to Black feminism in Toi Derricotte's beautiful poem, "The Telly Cycle."

of our time and attention is focused on instantaneous reaction, it seems almost inconceivable that nothing might be the best something we can offer."[33] And yet history suggests that it's sometimes the right move. Slowing down your reaction time can allow you to move *faster* as an organization, particularly when it helps you avoid unforced errors, a topic for tomorrow.

> **GUT CHECK:** Proceed when you're ready
> to tell a great change story.

FRIDAY

Go as Fast as You Can

On April 4, 1967, Dr. Martin Luther King Jr. spoke to a packed Riverside Church in Morningside Heights, a dynamic neighborhood on the Upper West Side of New York City. At this point, King was the most visible leader in the movement to advance civil rights in America. The focus of his speech that day was the Vietnam War, a subject many observers felt was "off topic."[1]

Breaking his official silence on the war, King made the politically risky decision to connect the conflict to the rest of his life's work. He urged Americans to engage with the war's true horror and social costs, not at some vague future point, but with the "fierce urgency of now," an electric phrase King had used in his "I Have a Dream" speech a few years earlier. "We are now faced with the fact that tomorrow is today," he thundered from Riverside's pulpit. "In this unfolding conundrum of life and history there is such a thing as being too late."[2]

There is such a thing as being too late. There are many staggering lines in this speech, but we always have to remind ourselves
to breathe after this one. The clock is ticking. The opportunity for
change is finite. It's not just what we do, but when we do it, that
makes the difference between admirable intentions and having
any impact at all. A year to the day after he gave this speech, King
was assassinated.

Friday is about not missing your chance to change things. The
payoff of all your hard work over the last week—all your efforts to
build trust and make new friends and tell your change story with
grace—is that you've now earned the right to move fast. You're
far more likely to pull it all off and far *less* likely to break things
along the way.

Your mission today is to execute your Very Good Plan with a
sense of urgency. We're going to use the word *urgency* without
apology, even though it's also suffered from speed's bad reputation and association with phenomena like "hustle culture."* But
urgency, at its best, cuts through the complexity and noise of
our organizational lives. It releases a system's energy and makes
it clear to everyone that the problem you're solving matters.
Urgency recognizes that *there is such a thing as being too late.*

In our experience, most big organizational problems deserve
a more urgent response, a metabolic rate that honors the frustration and mediocrity and—in many cases—the real pain of the
status quo. And so today you're going to strip out distractions,
update assumptions (as a starting place, see "Ten Beliefs That Get
in the Way of Moving Fast"), and launch yourself over whatever

---

*Urgency is a selective focus that enables fast, strategic action. Note that if everything
is urgent, as in hustle culture, then nothing is urgent.

FRIDAY'S AGENDA

1. Get out of the way.
2. Be bad at something else.
3. Become a culture warrior.*
4. Run better meetings.
5. Reduce work in process.
6. Create a way to fast-track projects.
7. Lean into conflict.

Materials You'll Need for Today

- Documentation of the key elements of your Very Good Plan
- Understanding of your organizational culture, aka *how things are really done around here*
- Willingness to share decision rights with people who have earned them
- Budget for serving delicious, nutritionally dense snacks to your team
- A piece of music that helps downshift your nervous system
- Self-awareness

---

administrative hurdles are in the way of making progress. People often ask us about the right timing for big change, and our answer is almost always the same: How about *now*? Now seems like a good time to accelerate excellence. TGIF.

*Someone who looks fearlessly at their organizational culture and knows they can change it.

Ten Beliefs That Get in the Way of Moving Fast

We're going to explore many of these themes in the pages ahead, but we want to create some tension up front and get you in touch with the likelihood that you or someone you love may be playing some role in unproductively lowering your organization's metabolic rate. Although speed bumps may manifest as external barriers to progress (Too many meetings! Byzantine approval protocols!), they start, like most things, as ideas and assumptions embedded in those internal, skull-size kingdoms we're still inhabiting, although hopefully with less enthusiasm by Friday.

1. **Meaningful change happens slowly.** When we view the human story from the luxury of distance, progress can take decades, generations, even centuries (or longer). History may take that long, but *change* can be measured in the minutes, hours, and days it takes to identify a problem and start the flywheel of action that leads ultimately to solutions. Indeed, if you look closely, history lurches forward when changemakers decide that the moment that matters most is *right now*.

2. **We can do it later.** The most successful change leaders we know are acutely aware of the cost of *not now*, the high price a system pays when it's static. They live the adage that comfortable inaction is riskier than uncomfortable action. In the national reckoning on justice and race that followed George Floyd's murder, Bill Valle, CEO of Fresenius Medical Care North America, stood up and essentially said to the organization, "I don't yet know exactly what we're going to do, but I know we have to start *now*."

He then moved quickly to empower a team to help build a stronger culture of belonging at the company.[3]

3. **Other people's time is an abundant, low-cost resource.** We're going to revisit this topic again here—just like we do in real life—whenever we get the chance. If you're in a leadership role, your colleagues' time is the most strategic resource you have the privilege of consuming. The leaders who get speed right treat that resource preciously by doing everything from helping their teams to prioritize ruthlessly to carefully planning and facilitating meetings. The leaders who don't get speed right tend to use other people's time casually.

4. **We need more information.** In a letter to Amazon shareholders, Jeff Bezos argued that most decisions should be made with about 70 percent of the information you want.[4] Some of the leaders we know who've stumbled in leading change were holding out for 100 percent of the information they wanted, including crystal ball confidence in the endings of stories not yet written—precisely how employees would react to a decision, for example, or how competitors would respond to a bold strategic move. It felt safer to these leaders to have more meetings and run more scenarios, but that sense of safety was illusory. All that waiting made the organization more vulnerable, not less.

5. **Going fast is reckless.** We'll defer to the rhetorical mastery of Ralph "Waldo" Emerson (he really did go by Waldo) for a more poetic way to say this. In his essay on the topic of *prudence*, he observed that "in skating over thin ice, our safety is our speed."[5] For those of you who are still suspicious of moving fast, keep this quote handy.

(continued)

A counterintuitive truth about speed is that it can make us safer rather than less safe by reducing our chances of falling through the metaphorical ice.

6. **Going slowly is righteous.** At the risk of repeating ourselves, we're going to say this another way: if you have not laid a strong foundation of trust, inclusion, and clarity (also known as Monday through Thursday), then please slow down and reassess. Take your foot off the accelerator and spend time in Responsible Stewardship. For everyone else, know that you're putting at risk your chance to make meaningful change. *There is such a thing as being too late.*

7. **Our people are stretched too thin.** Some of you may be slowing things down, even without realizing it, as an antidote to some other social or organizational ill such as anxiety, burnout, or distraction. When those feelings are showing up at scale in an organization, then downshifting is unlikely to help much. Return to Monday and deal *directly* with those problems. When leaders build trust by solving the right problems and taking care of their stakeholders, they can go as fast as their problems require.

8. **We have to be great at everything we do.** If you're unwilling to be bad at some things, then it means you're also unwilling to free up the resources—capital, time, energy—to truly excel at others.[6] If you want to overperform on *speed*, therefore, you'll have to underperform on some other organizational behavior. The trick is to choose something that both enables faster speed—to be bad *in the service of* great—and doesn't destroy trust with key stakeholders. This isn't as hard as it sounds, which we'll get into in the pages ahead.

9. **Structure is the enemy of speed.** The Navy Seals have a famous adage that "slow is smooth, and smooth is fast." We interpret this to mean, among other things, that while reducing friction can take some extra time in the near term, investment in process yields a faster pace on the other side. In our experience, creating good, clear operating systems is the best friction-reducing strategy available to you. At a minimum, make an agenda for your next meeting.

10. **We need more time to prepare.** Anticipation of change introduces anxiety into an ecosystem, and the antidote is to replace it with *actual* change. The longer you wait to lead change that's needed, the more time the humans around you have to *hallucinate*—a favorite term of our colleague Tom DeLong—about all the catastrophic turns the uncertain future could take. There's also rip-off-the-Band-Aid value to getting on with things that allows you to create momentum right out of the gate. As we've said before, *simply begin.*

Get Out of the Way

Many barriers to speed come down to relatively simple organizational physics. If you build a decision culture where all decision matter has to flow through a single point, then speed is going to be a very direct trade-off. Opening that aperture, even a little (for some of you, that means going from one to two key decision makers), can dramatically increase the tempo of your organization's "battle rhythm."

Here's a more aspirational way to say this: the fastest way to speed up your company is to empower more people to make more decisions. This can feel counterintuitive in industries where the stakes are high or where a chain of command is essential (in health care, for example), but it's when the stakes are highest that it's most important for your people to have the information they need to make the right calls without you. When conditions are slow-moving and predictable, sure, tell people what to do. In all other conditions, the safer bet is to teach them *how to think*.

It's no surprise, then, that some of the most compelling ideas on empowerment have emerged from the fog of war. When General Martin Dempsey, former chairman of the Joint Chiefs of Staff, set out to make the US Army faster and better, he started by *giving power away.*[7] Calling this new approach "Mission Command," Dempsey articulated a vision for army leadership focused on teaching subordinates how to make decisions on their own on the modern battlefield, where speed mattered more than ever and conditions were constantly shifting.*

For those of you still coming around to Dempsey's worldview, consider trying something new with your Very Good Plan. You worked hard yesterday to make your rigorous, optimistic change strategy clear and explain *why* you're doing what you're doing. Now let your team know which execution decisions—which *what* parts—won't require you. This is also an excellent time to discuss

---

*The leadership model Dempsey developed built on the ideas of a brilliant, nineteenth-century Prussian field marshal remembered as Helmuth von Moltke the Elder.

decision-making more broadly, tapping the wealth of decision frameworks out there to support you.[8] Most will push you to articulate when you want to be involved versus consulted versus briefed after-the-fact. Pick a framework and—you guessed it— run some intelligent experiments.

Today we're also going to invite you to lean into the *operations* of empowerment, structural changes that help to enable decentralized decision-making. One of our favorite examples is Ritz-Carlton's policy of giving every employee the power to spend up to $2,000 per incident to solve a guest problem on their own, no cumbersome manager approvals needed.[9] When asked about the policy, company founder Horst Shulze reflected: "When I introduced this practice years ago, the owners of Ritz-Carlton franchises threatened to sue me." Suppressing a smile, he pointed out that most incidents get resolved without going anywhere near the two-grand approval limit: "A plate of cookies or a lunch has sufficed."[10]

In our experience, many leaders either embrace or resist empowerment on an emotional level without fully thinking through the logic of it. That was Shulze's point to his skeptical franchise owners: "Even if we had spent the full $2,000, these are guests who are likely to spend $200,000 over their lives, so the only—*the only*—thing we should be concerned with is keeping them as guests."[11] This is before you even add in the word-of-mouth buzz the practice has created.

One story of a Ritz-Carlton employee "rescuing" a Thomas the Tank Engine toy for a guest's son has generated incalculable value in earned media.[12] The child lost the toy during the family's stay at a Ritz-Carlton property, and an enterprising employee made a trip to the toy store to replace it (estimated cost: $16.99). Before returning Thomas, the employee paused to photograph him in various spots in the hotel—prepping food in the kitchen, taking a refreshing morning swim—to explain Thomas's absence to his distraught young owner. This magical moment was made possible by an empowering, on-brand operating change and a corresponding line item to fund it.

In addition to speed, empowering your colleagues has other benefits, too, including better performance, higher job satisfaction, and greater interpersonal trust.[13] We interviewed decorated former Company Commander Emily Hannenberg about the impact of General Dempsey's newfangled leadership ideas. In her decade of military service, Hannenberg had distinguished herself spectacularly and was tapped to train new officers on Mission Command as a professor of military science at MIT. Hannenberg highlighted improved unit performance, morale, and, yes, speed, but she said the most notable difference was the way the model changed soldiers' perception of their abilities: "We moved faster, of course, but the biggest impact was confidence. When you're trusted to lead in your own spheres of influence, you discover you can do things you never imagined were possible. That changes your relationship with *yourself.*" In our less expert vocabulary, we'll put it this way: as you explore ways to empower your team, come for the speed, stay for the happy, unleashed colleagues.

> **GUT CHECK:** Proceed when you're ready to let other people make decisions that matter.

Dare to Be Bad at Something Else

It's a standing rule in the construction business that you can reasonably expect to get two of the following three things: cost, quality, speed. You can get good quality quickly, but it's going to cost you more. You can get something built fast and cheap, but the quality will suffer. Or you can get good quality for a competitive price, but you're going to have to wait for it. This is also known as the *impossible triangle.*

We love the impossible triangle not only because of our taste for three-pointed shapes, but because it's a very intuitive illustration of the trade-offs that make speed possible (and of strategic trade-offs more generally). If you're going to prioritize speed, then you're going to have to deprioritize something else. Said differently, in order to free up the resources to overdeliver on speed, you'll need to underdeliver on some other thing (the trick is to choose "some other thing" wisely). A major lesson of our decade of research on service companies—we wrote a book about this idea—is that organizations that resist and try to be great at everything usually end up in a state of "exhausted mediocrity."[14] Sound familiar?

One company that didn't resist was Southwest Airlines, which until recently was an exception to the rule that airlines must lose money and make their customers anxious and sad.[15] On its drive to becoming the most beloved airline in America, Southwest delivered best-in-class prices by choosing to be worst-in-class on other aspects of the flying experience. Speed was at the heart of this strategy. For example, by denying passengers some in-flight amenities (meals, assigned seats, a wide selection of beverages), Southwest could turn their planes around faster at the gate, which meant that the airline got more flying time out of its expensive airborne assets, which meant that it could charge lower prices—the thing its customers wanted most.[16] Southwest was bad, unapologetically bad, in the service of being great.

These kinds of decisions take courage, particularly for the achievement-oriented among us who do not like to disappoint people. Southwest's iconic cofounder and CEO Herb Kelleher once famously received a complaint letter from an angry grandmother, who was displeased with the company's policy of not transferring bags to other airlines.[17] The letter asked for the basic decency of helping her visit her grandkids without the hassle of dragging her luggage from one terminal to the next. It seemed like a reasonable request.

In Kelleher's response—a story he shared far and wide—he pointed out that Southwest's business model wouldn't survive if he reversed this policy. If his team had to pause in their turn-around sprints to deal with the complexity and uncertainty of another airline, then Southwest's speed (read: cost) advantage would disappear. Kelleher was very, very sorry, but he wouldn't be transferring this woman's bags anytime soon.

We love this story, enough to repeat it shamelessly in every book we write, because we can imagine how hard it would have been to say no to this woman. It would have been individually and organizationally painful to deny this loyal, sympathetic grandmother a basic service that every one of the company's cutthroat competitors offered. But in return for this kind of strategic discipline, Kelleher got to move faster than any other airline in history.

Which brings us back to our *impossible triangle*. In practice, the tool strengthens relationships because it enables a transparent discussion about the trade-offs of moving fast. Yes, we can prioritize speed, but something else has to give. Customers get to decide *before* the project begins whether that's a trade-off they want to make. In the same way that Kelleher leveled with Grandma about the terms of Southwest's deal, stakeholders get to make a clear-eyed decision about their own priorities. The alternative is to pretend you can be great at everything and lose trust as you go.

> **GUT CHECK:** Proceed when you're willing to accept your operating reality: to excel on speed, you must be bad at something else.

Become a Culture Warrior

Every successful change campaign we've had the privilege of being part of was defined by an acute awareness of time as a precious and perishable resource, the one truly nonrenewable resource the organization had. The campaign itself created an infectious momentum that tomorrow would be—tomorrow *had to be*—better than today. This culture of urgency was created the way culture is always created, by leaders who committed to a shared set of beliefs that then informed the actions they took.

Culture explains *how things are really done around here*. It tells us whether we should follow the rules or cut corners, whether we should share our unique knowledge or keep it to ourselves (remember Wednesday? We're now adding *fast* to your list of defining cultural attributes, in addition to *inclusiveness*), whether we should stick out our necks and try to improve things or keep our heads down and conform to the status quo. How important is it to move fast? What the boss said in the last staff meeting gives us some guidance, but it's culture that has the definitive answer.

There's still some disagreement about whether strategy—the kinds of trade-offs you made in the last section—or culture matters more. Management thinker Peter Drucker supposedly once said, "Culture eats strategy for breakfast," setting up a debate about which of the two is more powerful. In practice, culture usually wins this showdown, but only because strategy is rarely articulated well enough to influence the decision-making of most people in the company. Your job on Friday is to make it a fair fight by doing both well, by being a strategic leader who won't shut up about speed and its inevitable, unavoidable trade-offs—and by building an organizational culture that values *fast*.

One company that owes its success to that culture is FedEx. In 1973, FedEx was on the ropes, bankruptcy looming, nothing going right fast enough.[18] As this existential crisis unfolded, a FedEx customer called in tears because her wedding dress hadn't arrived yet, with less than twenty-four hours until the ceremony. A frontline employee named Diane (we've tried and failed to find her last name) jumped into action, tracked down the dress, and chartered a small Cessna to deliver it—all without wasting critical time by asking anyone for permission. This story got the attention of some executive guests at the wedding, who then decided to take a chance on a young, wobbly FedEx to ship some of their time-sensitive products. They drove enough new demand to save the company.

We like to tell and—yes, loyal *Unleashed* readers—to *retell* this story because it's such a beautiful illustration of the power of culture. This company-saving sequence of events was made possible because FedEx had built a strong, "bleeding purple" (the company's primary logo color) culture marked by a get-it-done ethos and disregard for status.[19] Everyone's contribution was valued. Everyone on the payroll had the freedom and responsibility to share their unique knowledge. Diane's bold choice created a lifeline for FedEx, and it was *culture* that compelled her to act.

As a starting place for getting in touch with how possible it is to change culture, we like the late management theorist Edgar Schein's seminal framework, which loosely divides organizational culture into artifacts, behaviors, and shared basic assumptions.[20] As Schein argues persuasively, to get people to reliably behave the way you want, you have to get them to reliably *think* the way you want. Again, ask yourself, "What must my smart, talented, gorgeous colleagues be *thinking* in order to be *acting* in ways that are slowing us down?"

If we refer back to our list from the beginning of the chapter ("Ten Beliefs That Get in the Way of Moving Fast"), they may be reacting to widespread burnout at the company or trying to be great at everything (bless them!) because they're convinced it's the right thing to do.* Simply telling them to go faster is only

---

*We hear this a lot from people working in mission-driven sectors, such as health care and education, who argue that it's their ethical obligation to at least try to be great at everything they do. We often respond by simply asking, "How's that working out for you?"

going to get you so far, even if you're the one in charge. The only chance you have of changing their behavior is to influence their beliefs. In the spirit of show-not-tell, what are some Tuesday-ish experiments you could run to evolve their thinking and get everyone to pick up the pace?

For the rest of this chapter, we'll be making suggestions, but we want to be clear that this work isn't just for companies seeking to compete *on* speed, such as Southwest and FedEx, but also companies seeking to compete *with* speed, which is the majority of people reading this book. For those of you in this second category, the most powerful tool you have to build momentum is culture. Schein once argued that "the only thing of real importance that leaders do is to create and manage culture." Wherever you happen to be in the hierarchy, on Friday add culture to your job description. Quietly add a "c" for culture to your title (no one has to know) and create an environment built on the belief that there is such a thing as being too late.

> **GUT CHECK:** Proceed when you're ready to take responsibility for building a culture of speed.

Run Better Meetings

Author and columnist Dave Barry once said, "If you had to identify, in one word, the reason why the human race has not achieved, and never will achieve, its full potential, that word would be 'meetings.'"[21] What makes the comment funny, like anything funny, is that there's something true at the core of it. We're now spending a full third of our working hours in meetings (three times as much as we did just a few years ago), and much of that time *hurts*.[22] One study found that more than two-thirds of workers reported that excessive meetings were distracting them from "making an impact at work," which is presumably what we're all there to do, and another estimated that across the United States, the United Kingdom, Germany, and Switzerland, pointless meetings were costing companies nearly *half a trillion dollars* annually.[23]

Many leaders have responded by simply banning this toxic substance (no-meeting Fridays!) without even trying to get better at what amounts to an essential organizational behavior. To kick off our speed experiments and help us up our meeting game, we invited Claire Hughes Johnson back into the conversation (recall her Tuesday cameo in our discussion of intelligent people experiments) since she is legendarily good at running meetings.* On the short list of leadership strengths that explains Hughes Johnson's extraordinary track record, she includes "meeting structure," in addition to less surprising items like clear goals and metrics.[24] Despite the centrality of meetings to our work lives, we've never heard another senior leader identify them as critical to their success. When we asked Hughes Johnson about it, she put it this way: "Your most productive, highest-impact work is with other humans in real time . . . that's called a meeting."[25]

Hughes Johnson's principal advice is to invest in preparation. Before you have the audacity to convene people, have answers to these key questions: *Why are we meeting? What are our objectives? Who needs to be there to achieve these objectives? How are we going to spend our time together?* Circulate materials in advance so that

---

*A casual talk Hughes Johnson gave in 2018 on how to run an effective staff meeting immediately went viral.

everyone has the runway to contribute effectively, which some people need more than others. "Extroverts talk to think," Hughes Johnson explained. "Introverts think to talk."[26] Always create an agenda, which both signals where you're going and keeps everyone on track. Annette Catino, founder and former chief executive of QualCare Alliance Networks, is one of many executives who won't gather without one: "If I don't have an agenda in front of me, I walk out . . . if I don't know why we're in the meeting, and you don't know why we're there, then there's no reason for a meeting."[27]

Once the meeting begins, consider sharing the challenge of meeting management with other people in the room. At Stripe, Hughes Johnson would often deputize a notetaker and sometimes a facilitator, particularly for the most important meetings, to help her promote full engagement in the room. If someone in the meeting was hanging back or seemed reluctant to participate, the facilitator was empowered to slow down the discussion and skillfully invite in new voices. Author and gathering expert Priya Parker goes even further, suggesting you assign roles and even playful titles to *anyone* who can help you accomplish your objectives, from a "Dean of Water" to a special "connective-tissue role" to culture builders who can help you create community.[28] Another tactic we use is to challenge *everyone* in the room to index on empathy and be prepared to co-produce a good outcome even if it's not "their" meeting.

These approaches can also help you elicit unique information from your fellow gatherers, a central goal of inclusion—and of good meeting management. As we explored in our discussion of inclusive meetings on Wednesday, find out what happens when you use our favorite prompt: "Can someone *articulate* a different point of view?" which is a lower-stakes variant of "Who *has* a different point of view?" This will also help you to engage in divergent thinking—a healthy exploration of different ideas and options—before converging too quickly on a less-than-optimal solution. In our experience, fast convergence typically leads to *a false optima* (also known as *not our best idea)* and a lower likelihood that people will be willing to interrupt the meeting and offer a new idea, even if it's a better one.

Finally, stick the landing. Before your meeting ends, summarize key decisions and action items. Make sure everyone knows what they're responsible for delivering and the deadlines they need to hit. Hughes Johnson likes to use a "check-out" at the close of meetings—a rapid-fire prompt to help reinforce commitments and get a pulse check on the group's experience. Two she uses regularly are "Share one thing you will commit to after this meeting" and "Use one or two words to describe what you're thinking as we close this meeting—it could be a feeling, an idea, a topic you want more of."

As with all of our guidance, we urge you to get into the organizational sandbox and *play* with new approaches. Are you gathering to ideate or execute? Learn from what just happened or prepare for what's coming? Adapt your meeting's structure, style, and pace to your goals, whether it's to generate creative options or to get everyone on the same operating page. For example, borrow from the Agile software development toolkit and meet briefly once a day to remove roadblocks to progress (the true believers do this standing up to promote efficiency, hence the term of art, *stand-up*) . . . or don't do that because it makes no sense for what you're trying to achieve collectively. The only truly universal rule is that if you're gathering in person for any significant amount of time, then you need to feed people real food, which is why we asked you to pack good snacks today.

The point, in short, is to spend time preparing before you assemble anyone to do *anything*. In her best-selling ode to the lost art of gathering, Parker writes, "When we don't examine the deeper assumptions behind why we gather, we end up . . . replicating old, staid formats of gathering. And we forgo the possibility of creating something memorable, even transformative."[29] What would happen if you aimed for memorable, even *transformative* the next time you called a meeting?

With relatively minimal effort, we've seen companies go from sixty-minute meetings to thirty-minute meetings, thirty-minute meetings to twenty-minute meetings, using our preferred intervention profile: no new people, no new technology, just a healthy dose of deliberate effort and training. Indeed, it's the simplest way to build speed in an organization. If you do nothing else, run better meetings.

> **GUT CHECK:** Proceed when you've committed to bring more intention to meetings.

Remove Work in Process

Before we go any further, Frances would like us to pause and "remind" readers of Little's Law, her favorite operations principle.* Here's the punch line: If you want to increase the speed of

*You may notice a slight shift in authorial voice in this section.

your team or organization, don't just focus on how fast you're all moving. Also pay attention to how many things you're trying to do. In fact, when it comes to picking up the pace, the length of your collective to-do list not only matters, *it matters just as much* (gasp!) as how quickly you're ticking things off.

In his groundbreaking research on queueing theory in the 1950s, legendary operations professor John Little discovered that the start-to-finish time of an item in a system (e.g., a person waiting in line) is equal to the number of items (can we please just call them people?) in the queue and the time it takes to complete each item (pay for your stuff and go).[30] For example, if you get in line at Starbucks and there are three people ahead of you, and it takes two minutes for the barista to take a Frappuccino order and swipe a credit card, then you will spend eight minutes in line: four people multiplied by two minutes per person to check out.

When we write this out as an equation, it looks like this:

Start-to-finish time = Work in process × Cycle time

Reflecting on this equation, which we're all of course doing, we can see that there are two ways to improve start-to-finish time. We can either reduce work in process (WIP) or speed up cycle time. Most of us instinctually try to speed up cycle time by asking people to work harder and faster. But this approach ignores the power of reducing WIP, also known as working *smarter*.

When Josh Silverman, CEO of Etsy, was turning the company around, he concluded that too many projects were "suffocating" the organization. Although Etsy had a staff of fewer than a thousand, the team was working on more than eight hundred business development projects. Silverman and his team eliminated half of these initiatives, applying Little's Law to the activities of the entire organization. They gained critical speed by making an org-level commitment to work smarter.[31]

Here's the kicker on this part of the story, which we promise to wrap up momentarily. WIP is usually a much larger variable than cycle time, while also being operationally easier to reduce in most systems. If your goal is to speed up a checkout process, for example, reducing the number of people in line is smarter than trying to shave seconds off the checkout experience. According to Professor Little's breakthrough math, you'll gain a lot more velocity by creating a second checkout line than by asking your cashiers to get a move on it.

Could the news get any better? Readers, the answer is yes. Eliminating WIP is also often a onetime effort. As long as Etsy resists the mission creep of new projects—a discipline it's likely to have on Silverman's watch—then the company gets to maintain its new speed. Your own inbox is a good analog. To improve your email response time, don't learn to type faster; clear out the backlog once and for all. Work smarter, not harder. And then urgently execute your Very Good Plan by reducing the number of *other* things you're doing today.

> **GUT CHECK:** Proceed when you're ready to reduce the amount of work in process, which you can now confidently refer to as "WIP."

Create a Way to Fast-Track Projects

After embracing the life-changing magic of Little's Law, Silverman's next move at Etsy was to rapidly accelerate the company's most important projects. Many of these projects were simple product fixes with the best chance of boosting sales quickly. For example, many Etsy shoppers were nervous about using their credit cards with small, unknown vendors they didn't yet trust, so the company prioritized adding a message to the site: "The seller never sees your credit card information."[32] Silverman called these fixes *ambulances* and focused the team on implementing them in days and weeks rather than months.[33] His ambulances paid off with an almost-immediate increase to revenues.[34]

An ambulance is an unpleasant metaphor, but it makes the point in brutally memorable language. Push the less essential tasks to the side of the road to make room for the ones that matter most. Many of the organizations in Accelerating Excellence we've studied have developed ambulance-like devices to make this kind of prioritization easier (at Stripe, these projects were called "Code Yellow"), an approach that can be applied to any problem, not just product fixes—and to organizations of all shapes, sizes, and degrees of entrenched bureaucracy.

Our colleagues Amy Edmondson and Ranjay Gulati have been studying how large companies can adopt the values of Agile software development, which we would argue is a methodology that's designed fundamentally to move fast and fix things.[35] Agile's principles emphasize rapid prototyping, quick adaptation, and continuous, empowered dialogue among stakeholders. One finding in Edmondson and Gulati's work is that while bureaucracy has its place (and often gets a bad rap), even large, established companies need to bypass it some of the time in pursuit of speed, flexibility, and innovation. In these circumstances, it can help to use what they call "agility hacks."[36]

Like Silverman's ambulances, agility hacks allow you to speed past the rest of your WIP and anything else in the way of your objective. For many organizations, particularly later-stage companies, agility hacks have the added benefit of not disrupting whatever else the organization is doing. You simply cruise around it. Edmondson and Gulati share wonderful examples, and we encourage you to read their work directly for ideas and inspiration.[37]

One of our favorite agility hacks they describe is when the global pharmaceutical giant Novartis decided to *bypass* (there's that word again) its own R&D processes by launching a high-profile, fast-paced innovation contest called Project Genesis. The competition invited cross-disciplinary teams to pitch ideas for moonshot projects to a panel of the company's top scientists. The winning team got lab space, funding, and eighteen months to develop their ideas further. At the end of this period, teams that were making good progress joined one of Novartis's existing R&D programs.[38]

One of the contest winners commented, "I am surprised by how much Genesis speeds things up. We were able to get prime lab space and equipment in just a couple of weeks"—a remarkable timeline for Big Biotech.[39] We love this comment, in part, because of this seemingly mundane operational detail, the way the contest created a better, more efficient marketplace for *office space.* It makes sense for a company like Novartis to quickly allocate resources to potentially transformative technologies and therapeutics—and yet without a way to fast-track projects, it can take an excruciating amount of time for any organization to get this right.

> **GUT CHECK:** Proceed when you're curious about creating a mechanism to accelerate high-impact priorities.

Lean into Conflict

As we close out the week, we want to go after one final speed bump that's often hidden from view: how your organization deals with conflict. In a recent study, our colleague Francesca Gino found that nearly 60 percent of respondents described disagreements at work as "moderately, very, or extremely unpleasant." More than a third said they preferred to avoid them, and even more thought they were "destructive to their professional relationships and productivity."[40] In our own experience, an unskilled relationship with conflict is among the primary obstacles to Accelerating Excellence. It vacuums up energy, erodes trust, and slows everything way down.

Another way to think about this is that many levers of speed—including many of the items on your agenda today—require you to engage productively with conflict. *Someone's* feathers are going to get ruffled when you choose to underperform in their area of expertise or to speed past one of their beloved projects you're now treating as nonessential WIP. When you mismanage conflicts like these, you unintentionally hit the organizational breaks. You divert resources from your most urgent priorities and increase the likelihood of future cleanup and rework. One CEO we advised admitted to buying a company just to avoid a direct confrontation with his CFO. We hear stories like this all the time, and the cost to organizations is staggering.

The buildup of undiscussed and unresolved issues is a phenomenon that team-effectiveness expert Liane Davey calls "conflict debt."[41] We love this term because it both describes the burden of conflict avoidance and reinforces the solvability of it. Like tech debt, conflict debt is an org-level problem that's highly fixable with capable and intentional focus.

There are many fantastic resources out there to help you reduce conflict debt and manage interpersonal friction more effectively. *Crucial Conversations*, now on its third edition, sets readers up for success in discussions where "(1) stakes are high, (2) opinions vary, and (3) emotions run strong," a nexus that describes your most important decisions at work.[42] Kim Scott's *Radical Candor* builds on these ideas and shows us how to deliver tough feedback—a specific type of *crucial conversation*—that builds trust and actually helps people improve.[43] Chris Argyris laid the groundwork with his research on learning organizations and the value of "discussing the undiscussable," a phrase we think about at least once a day in our work.[44]

Some of you, we know, are getting uncomfortable just *thinking* about conflict. If your pulse is starting to quicken, then put on some of that calming music and use these resources to create a rigorous personal improvement plan. In our experience coaching conflict-averse leaders, reading about healthy responses to work conflict can be a kind of low-stakes exposure therapy that allows you to visualize all parties coming out ahead in the end, even when there's significant discomfort along the way. The practice is also a good reminder that conflict management is a *learned* behavior. A first step is to recognize it as an essential leadership skill, one we have to develop like any other—and also cultivate in our colleagues.

When new employees join Intel, their onboarding training includes learning about different conflict-management tools. The training sets the expectation that conflict is a normal part of collaboration, while also giving people a common language to discuss and resolve it.[45] L'Oréal offers employees a program called Managing Confrontation, which teaches participants how to disagree skillfully in a meeting (that place where your most productive, highest-impact work happens). Among other benefits, the program has helped the global cosmetics giant to navigate conflict norms that can diverge meaningfully across different cultures and markets.[46]

We once heard a senior leader, a woman thriving at the apex of the sharp-elbowed private equity industry, describe skilled conflict management as "comfort with tournament play." The medieval metaphor works for us, in part, because of the word *play*. The chemicals that conflict dumps into our bloodstream—often a potent cocktail of cortisol and testosterone—shock us into thinking that the stakes are high, but we're usually misreading the situation. This is the point that banking veteran Matt Trombley makes in his work on "agonism," which he defines as taking a warlike stance in situations that do not require it.[47] Some lightness in the jousting saddle can go a long way.

Today we want you to reject agonism and invoke the spirit of a low-key, low-stakes Renaissance Festival—the perfect outing for a Friday afternoon—and consider reframing conflict in your organization as *not such a bad thing*.* There's persuasive research out there that some types of conflict may actually help people stay engaged in their jobs and use the full scope of their intelligence.[48] In a longitudinal study, researchers found that high-performing teams often had high levels of disagreement about how to do their work.[49]

Conflict is also an essential ingredient in innovation, as our colleague Linda Hill has shown. Hill introduced the world to the gracious concept of "creative abrasion," the process by which potential solutions are created, explored, and modified through healthy debate and disagreement. Hill makes the case that excellence actually *requires* conflict between different ideas and approaches. As Jim Morris, the president of Pixar Animation Studios, told Hill, "If you have no conflict, you're going to have something that's pretty average."[50]

The most encouraging research we've seen comes from the desk of conflict expert and opinion writer Amanda Ripley. In a recent piece on unexpected pockets of productivity in the US Congress, a place where it often seems like the pace has slowed to the speed of *backward*, Ripley told the story of rapid progress made by the Select Committee on the Modernization of Congress.[51] Despite its set-up-to-fail design (six Republicans, six Democrats) and cumbersome voting requirements (a supermajority of members' votes

---

*We would like to formally retract any past "definition of hell" comments we made about attending a Renaissance Festival.

was required to do anything), the committee became one of the highest-functioning entities in Congress, creating what one *Roll Call* reporter called a "parallel congressional universe."[52]

To achieve this unexpected outcome, Committee Chairman Representative Derek Kilmer (D-Wash.) did unconventional things like host a bipartisan retreat—an almost unheard-of move—and build one shared staff team to support the committee's work rather than two smaller partisan teams. He *ran better meetings* by using roundtable formats for committee meetings and made Democrats and Republicans sit next to each other. He encouraged the committee to *discuss the undiscussable*, including what each member had experienced on January 6, both the personal pain of it and the starkly different views of the day's horrors from Republican and Democratic vantage points. Progress was possible because Kilmer worked *with* conflict rather than *around* it, running countless experiments in how to approach committee leadership in a new way. Committee Vice Chairman William Timmons (R-S.C.) summed it up this way: "We actually spent time together, and we talked about things." The payoff was a team that moved faster and fixed more things than any other committee in Congress.[53]

The last tactical thing we want you to do this week is to spend time with your colleagues and talk about things, particularly the colleagues with whom you disagree. By the end of the day, your Even Better Plan will have a chance of becoming A Great Plan.

> **GUT CHECK:** Proceed when you're
> ready to go as fast as you can.

CONCLUSION

TAKE THE WEEKEND OFF

Congratulations! Whether you stuck intrepidly to our five-day agenda or customized the timeline to your own needs, you just did something difficult and ambitious. You changed the *way things are done around here*. You refused to let the past dictate the future. The only work that remains is to rest and recover (more on that topic in a minute). Pour yourself another adult beverage as we finish up here.

At the beginning of this adventure, we promised that if you followed our playbook, you would now have a road map to Accelerating Excellence and be cruising toward your goals at an exhilarating speed. So how'd we do? Is the open road calling, or is it still hard to see around the next bend? Before you answer, let's do a quick review of what you accomplished this week:

On *Monday*, you identified your real problem. You asked tough questions, built a team of problem solvers, and surfaced a major roadblock to progress. You gathered new data and you listened, *really* listened, with the curiosity of an anthropologist and the accountability of a leader.

On *Tuesday*, you solved for trust. With confidence that you were solving the right problem, you ran smart experiments in how to steady your company's trust *wobbles* and strengthened your relationships with key stakeholders. You climbed into your organizational sandbox and *played*.

On *Wednesday*, you made new friends. You created the conditions for other people to thrive, not in spite of their differences as complex, multidimensional humans, but precisely *because* of those differences. You designed a better change plan—and became a better team—by including more and more varied perspectives.

On *Thursday*, you told a good story. You honored the past (both the good stuff and the not-so-good), articulated a compelling change mandate, and described a rigorous and optimistic way forward. You told your story, again and again, and you put your emotions to work.

On *Friday*, you went as fast as you could. You led change with a sense of urgency, empowering others to execute quickly—and at a reduced risk of breaking things. You dared to be bad, became a culture warrior, and decided that *there is such a thing as being too late*.

Do you wish you had taken longer or done less? Think back to where you placed your organization on the FIX map (figure C-1) at the beginning of the week. Now compare that assessment with where you are now. How much faster did you go than your company's typical pace? How much more did you accomplish?

FIGURE C-1

FIX map

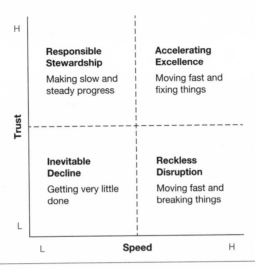

Most important, what happened next? Which destinations came into view that seemed unreachable even a "week" ago? We care a lot about trust and speed, but what we care most about is whatever change you seek to lead inside your organization—and, for some of you, well beyond it. For all our quadrants and shapes and dials, what we're really trying to measure is *possibility*. Did change feel more possible Friday afternoon than it did on Monday morning? If so, then this week was a wild success.

Travelers, your task now is to rest. For those of you who are reluctant to exhale, we're going to refer you to peak performance researchers, Jim Loehr and Tony Schwartz, who have been on a decades-long mission to get high achievers to take breaks. In their work studying elite athletes, Loehr and Schwartz determined that "the real enemy of high performance is not stress . . .

the problem is the absence of disciplined intermittent recovery."[1] The main lesson we take from their breakthrough insight is the importance of combining high effort with deep renewal—sprint with recovery—which is also important for the *organizational* body. The expanded version of our playbook, then, is to move fast, fix things, and rest. Start the cycle again once you've recovered your life force. It's one reason we like using the week as a metaphorical structure for change leadership. A week, it turns out, is always followed by a weekend.

How do you know when it's time for a break? Loehr and Schwartz will tell you to plan for it, to build recovery into your schedule as rigorously as you've designed and executed your good-to-great change plan. Our friend Arianna Huffington will urge you not to wait for a crisis.[2] Tricia Hersey of Nap Ministry fame will push you to take rest wherever you can get it, particularly if you don't yet have full control over your time.[3] We often invite Mary Oliver to keep us honest on this one with her soul-piercing question, "Listen, are you breathing just a little, and calling it a life?"[4]

We're now going to model good behavior and let you get on with your weekend. And whenever you're ready to begin again—whenever you're ready to call it Monday morning—remember this: there's a relationship that's wobbly at the center of any problem you're having. Find out what happens when you move fast to fix it and decide that the moment that matters most is *now*.

GLOSSARY

Accelerating Excellence *n*: the practice of moving fast and fixing things

anchor *n*: a stable pillar of trust, either authenticity, empathy, or logic

awesome *adj*: exceptionally positive and/or capable; *used sparingly outside the United States*

belonging *n*: the experience of feeling authentically connected to a team and/or organization; substitute for *inclusion*

can-do lesbian spirit *n*: the energy and confidence to improve things

capable *adj*: the ability to meet customer needs

co-production *n*: when two or more groups of people participate in production; in services, employees *and* customers are involved in production. In manufacturing, in contrast, only employees produce goods.

culture warrior *n*: someone who looks fearlessly at their organizational culture and knows they can change it

DEI *n*: the formal practice of advancing diversity, equity, and inclusion inside an organization

devotion *n*: full-bodied, unapologetic commitment to someone else's success

Even Better Plan *n*: intentional, subsequent iterations of a Good Enough Plan

in control *adj*: the ability to produce consistent outcomes

Inclusion Dial *n*: an individual's progressive experience of workplace belonging on a scale from safe to championed

indignities list *n*: a summary of barriers to employee performance that appear small but collectively undermine the achievement, engagement, and dignity of your colleagues

Inevitable Decline *n*: the practice of getting very little done

intelligent failure *n*: an unsuccessful attempt to achieve something

Good Enough Plan *n*: a collection of pilot projects that build trust and speed simultaneously, precursor to an Even Better Plan

leadership *n*: the practice of enabling and empowering others, in both your presence and absence; *also* creating the conditions for other people to thrive (colloquial)

love *v*: to set high standards and reveal deep devotion simultaneously

Monday morning questions *n*: conversational prompts that help to surface barriers to organizational performance

problem *n*: a significant barrier to organizational progress; may also be described as an *issue* or (less intuitively) *opportunity*

Reckless Disruption *n*: the practice of moving fast and breaking things

Responsible Stewardship *n*: the practice of making slow and steady progress

Sunday night data *n*: existing organizational data, before performing additional analytics

thump *v*: to compete and win in dramatic fashion

trust *n*: the willingness to rely on the words and/or actions of a person, team, or organization

Tuesday morning confidence *n*: the conviction as a leader that you are distinguishing clearly between activity and impact

urgency *n*: selective focus that enables fast, strategic action

Very Good Plan *n*: intentional, subsequent iterations of an Even Better Plan

wobble *n*: an unstable pillar of trust, in either authenticity, empathy, or logic

NOTES

INTRODUCTION

1. Frances Frei and Anne Morriss, *Unleashed: The Unapologetic Leader's Guide to Empowering Everyone Around You* (Boston: Harvard Business Review Press, 2020).

2. Facebook, Form S-1 (filed February 1, 2012), via SEC, https://www.sec.gov /Archives/edgar/data/1326801/000119312512034517/d287954ds1.htm.

CHAPTER 1

1. Francesca Gino, *Rebel Talent: Why It Pays to Break the Rules at Work and Life* (New York: Dey Street Books, 2018).

2. "Hershey CEO Michele Buck on Empowering Internal Change Agents," interview by Adi Ignatius, *Harvard Business Review* digital article, April 19, 2022, https://hbr.org/2022/04/hershey-ceo-michele-buck-on-empowering -internal-change-agents.

3. "Hershey CEO Michele Buck."

4. Rob Reed, "The Kat Cole Story: Unlikely Success at the Intersection of Hooters and Cinnabon," *Forbes*, August 26, 2020, https://www.forbes.com/sites /robreed/2020/08/26/the-kat-cole-story-unlikely-success-at-the-intersection -of-hooters-and-cinnabon/.

5. Interview with Christine Keung, March 10, 2023.

6. Interview with AJ Hubbard, February 10, 2022.

7. One gift of the past few decades of strategy scholarship is that a number of excellent frameworks for generating insight into your company's strategic position are now easily accessible in the public domain. Our favorites include *attribute maps* and *value stick analysis*, along with any other ideas developed by our colleague Felix Oberholzer-Gee, author of *Better, Simpler Strategy* (Boston: Harvard Business Review Press, 2021).

8. Joly has captured the full story, along with other great leadership advice, in his excellent book, *The Heart of Business: Leadership Principles for the Next Era of Capitalism* (Boston: Harvard Business Review Press, 2021).

9. Michael S. Hopkins, "Scott Cook, Intuit because He Learns, and Teaches," *Inc.*, February 6, 2020, https://www.inc.com/magazine/20040401/25cook.html.

10. Geoff Colvin, "How Intuit Reinvents Itself," *Fortune*, November 1, 2017, https://fortune.com/2017/10/20/how-intuit-reinvents-itself/.

11. Yuki Nogushi, "Health Workers Know What Good Care Is. Pandemic Burnout Is Getting in the Way," NPR, October 2, 2017, https://www.npr.org /sections/healt-shots/2021/10/02/1039312524/health-workers-know-what -good-care-is-pandemic-burnout-is-getting-in-the-way.

CHAPTER 2

1. David Foster Wallace, *This Is Water: Some Thoughts, Delivered on a Significant Occasion, about Living a Compassionate Life* (New York: Little, Brown, 2009), 117.

2. Amy C. Edmondson and Hanna Rodriguez-Farrar, "The Electric Maze Exercise," Harvard Business School Exercise 604–046, October 2003 (rev. January 2004).

3. For an exhilarating explanation of intelligent failure, see Amy C. Edmondson, *Right Kind of Wrong: The Science of Failing Well* (New York: Atria Books, 2023).

4. Jake Gibson, "Celebrating Failure: How to Make a Hit out of Misses," *Entrepreneur*, March 19, 2014, https://www.entrepreneur.com/growing-a -business/celebrating-failure-how-to-make-a-hit-out-of-misses/232323.

5. Gibson, "Celebrating Failure."

6. Michael Schrage, *The Innovator's Hypothesis: How Cheap Experiments Are Worth More Than Good Ideas* (Cambridge, MA: MIT Press, 2014), 60.

7. Frances Frei and Anne Morriss, *Unleashed: The Unapologetic Leader's Guide to Empowering Everyone Around You* (Boston: Harvard Business Review Press, 2020).

8. Leslie Hook, "Can Uber Ever Make Money?," Uber Technologies, *Financial Times*, June 22, 2017, https://www.ft.com/content/09278d4e -579a-11e7-80b6-9bfa4c1f83d2.

9. Sheelah Kolhatkar, "At Uber, a New C.E.O. Shifts Gears," *New Yorker*, March 30, 2018, https://www.newyorker.com/magazine/2018/04/09/at-uber -a-new-ceo-shifts-gears; Dara Khosrowshahi, "A New Future for Uber and Grab in Southeast Asia," Uber Newsroom, March 26, 2018, https://www.uber.com /newsroom/uber-grab/.

10. Mike Ettore, "Why Most New Executives Fail—and Four Things Companies Can Do About It," *Forbes*, March 13, 2020, https://www.forbes.com /sites/forbescoachescouncil/2020/03/13/why-most-new-executives-fail-and -four-things-companies-can-do-about-it/.

11. Jeff Feng, Erin Coffman, and Elena Grewal, "How Airbnb Democratizes Data Science with Data University," *Medium*, May 24, 2017, https://medium .com/airbnb-engineering/how-airbnb-democratizes-data-science-with-data -university-3eccc71e073a.

12. Alessandro Di Fiore, "Why AI Will Shift Decision Making from the C-Suite to the Front Line," *Harvard Business Review*, August 3, 2018, https:// hbr.org/2018/08/why-ai-will-shift-decision-making-from-the-c-suite-to -the-frontline.

13. Stuart Dredge, "Steve Jobs Resisted Third-Party Apps on iPhone, Biography Reveals," *Guardian*, October 24, 2011, https://www.theguardian .com/technology/appsblog/2011/oct/24/steve-jobs-apps-iphone; "The App Store Turns 10," press release, Apple website, July 5, 2018, https://www.apple.com /newsroom/2018/07/app-store-turns-10/.

14. Frances Frei and Anne Morriss, *Uncommon Service: How to Win by Putting Customers at the Core of Your Business* (Boston: Harvard Business Review Press, 2012).

15. Ryan W. Buell, Robert S. Huckman, and Sam Travers, "Improving Access at VA," Case 617-012, (Harvard Business School, Boston, November 2016 [rev. August 2020]).

16. Elizabeth A. Harris, "How Barnes & Noble Went from Villain to Hero," *New York Times*, April 15, 2022, https://www.nytimes.com/2022/04/15/arts /barnes-noble-bookstores.html.

17. "Neither Entitled nor Titled: Why We Have No Titles at Gusto," press release, Gusto website, March 28, 2016, https://gusto.com/company-news /why-we-have-no-titles.

18. "Neither Entitled nor Titled."

19. Ryan Roslansky, "LinkedIn CEO Ryan Roslansky: 'Your Next Best Employee Is Most Likely Your Current Employee,'" *Fortune*, March 20, 2023, https://fortune.com/2023/03/20/linkedin-ceo-ryan-roslansky-best-employee -careers-leadership-tech/.

20. Matthew Bidwell, "Paying More to Get Less: Specific Skills, Matching, and the Effects of External Hiring versus Internal Promotion," *Administrative Science Quarterly* 56, no. 3 (2011): 369–407.

21. Michael P. Jeffries, "The Remarkable Rise of Tiffany Haddish," *Atlantic*, September 7, 2017, https://www.theatlantic.com/entertainment /archive/2017/09/the-remarkable-rise-of-tiffany-haddish/538872/.

22. Claire Hughes Johnson, *Scaling People: Tactics for Management and Company Building* (San Francisco: Stripe Press, 2023).

23. Frei and Morriss, *Unleashed*.

24. Our HBS colleagues have done wonderful work on the impact of layoffs. This is a great place to start: Sandra J. Sucher and Shalene Gupta, "Layoffs That Don't Break Your Company," *Harvard Business Review*, May–June 2018.

25. Kolhatkar, "At Uber, a New C.E.O. Shifts Gears"; Khosrowshahi, "A New Future for Uber and Grab in Southeast Asia."

26. Gloria Steinem, *My Life on the Road* (New York: Random House, 2015).

27. Hamdi Ulukaya, "The Anti-CEO Playbook," speech given at TED, April 2019.

28. "Patagonia's Next Chapter: Earth Is Now Our Only Shareholder," press release, Patagonia website, September 14, 2022, https://www .patagoniaworks.com/press/2022/9/14/patagonias-next-chapter-earth-is -now-our-only-shareholder.

29. Harris Insights & Analytics, "2022 Axios Harris Poll 100," PowerPoint Presentation, 2022.

30. Lauren Aratani, "'We've Lost the Right to Be Pessimistic': Patagonia Treads Fine Line Tackling Climate Crisis as For-Profit Company," *Guardian*, March 12, 2023, https://www.theguardian.com/business/2023/mar/12 /patagonia-climate-crisis-for-profit-company; Shelley E. Kohan, "Patagonia's Bold Move Shakes Up the Ideas of Capitalism and Consumerism," *Forbes*, September 15, 2022, https://www.forbes.com/sites/shelleykohan/2022/09/15 /patagonias-bold-move-shakes-up-the-ideas-of--capitalism-and-consumerism /?sh=121bab624518.

31. He's made this easier by writing a terrific book, *Let My People Go Surfing: The Education of a Reluctant Businessman* (New York: Penguin Books, 2006).

32. Sara Fischer, "Tech Firms' Big Trust Gap," Axios, May 25, 2022, https://www.axios.com/2022/05/25/tech-firms-big-trust-gap-harris-reputation-survey; Jeff Horwitz, "Facebook Says Its Rules Apply to All. Company Documents Reveal a Secret Elite That's Exempt," *Wall Street Journal*, September 13, 2021, https://www.wsj.com/articles/facebook-files-xcheck-zuckerberg-elite-rules-11631541353?mod=hp_lead_pos7.

33. Michael Bartiromo and Nexstar Media Wire, "Airline Passenger Claims United Was 'Lying' about Lost Luggage after AirTag Showed It at 'Mystery' Building," *Hill*, January 3, 2023, https://thehill.com/homenews/nexstar_media_wire/3796854-airline-passenger-claims-united-was-lying-about-lost-luggage-after-airtag-showed-it-at-mystery-building/.

CHAPTER 3

1. Henrik Bresman and Amy C. Edmondson, "Research: To Excel, Diverse Teams Need Psychological Safety," *Harvard Business Review*, March 17, 2022, https://hbr.org/2022/03/research-to-excel-diverse-teams-need-psychological-safety.

2. Kara Swisher, "There Is a Reason Tech Isn't Safe," *New York Times*, December 13, 2019, https://www.nytimes.com/2019/12/13/opinion/uber-silicon-valley.html.

3. David Gigone and Reid Hastie, "The Common Knowledge Effect: Information Sharing and Group Judgment," *Journal of Personality and Social Psychology* 65, no. 5 (1993): 959–974, doi: 10.1037/0022-3514.65.5.959.

4. Randall S. Peterson and Heidi K. Gardner, "Is Your Board Inclusive—or Just Diverse?" *Harvard Business Review*, September 28, 2022, https://hbr.org/2022/09/is-your-board-inclusive-or-just-diverse.

5. Starbucks, "'I Want People to Feel Like They Belong': Starbucks I&D Chief Dennis Brockman Focuses on Ultimate Goal," https://stories.starbucks.com/stories/2022/starbucks-i-and-d-chief-dennis-brockman-focuses-on-ultimate-goal/.

6. Robert Reiss, "I Asked the World's Top CEOs if They're Taking Diversity Seriously. Here's Why Their Answers Could Change Your Life," *Fortune*, November 23, 2022, https://fortune.com/2022/11/23/world-top-ceos-diversity-seriously-careers-workplace-leadership-robert-reiss/.

7. Sylvia Ann Hewlett and Kenji Yoshino, "LGBT-Inclusive Companies Are Better at 3 Big Things," *Harvard Business Review*, February 2, 2016, https://hbr.org/2016/02/lgbt-inclusive-companies-are-better-at-3-big-things; "What Job Seekers Really Think about Your Diversity and Inclusion Stats," Glassdoor for Employers, July 12, 2021, https://www.glassdoor.com/employers/blog/diversity/; Jennifer Miller, "For Younger Job Seekers, Diversity and Inclusion in the Workplace Aren't a Preference. They're a Requirement," *Washington Post*, February 18, 2021, https://www.washingtonpost.com/business/2021/02/18/millennial-genz-workplace-diversity-equity-inclusion/.

8. Karen Brown, "To Retain Employees, Focus on Inclusion—Not Just Diversity," *Harvard Business Review Digital Articles,* December 4, 2018, https://hbr.org/2018/12/to-retain-employees-focus-on-inclusion-not-just-diversity;

Jonathan S. Leonard and David I. Levine, "The Effect of Diversity on Turnover: A Large Case Study," *ILR Review* 59, no. 4 (2006): 547–572; SHRM Foundation, "Why Hire a Vet? The Business Case for Hiring Military Veterans," 2017, https://www.shrm.org/foundation/ourwork/initiatives/engaging-and-integrating-military-veterans/Documents/13056-G-01_SHRMF_WhyHireVet.pdf.

9. Josh Bersin, "Why Diversity and Inclusion Will Be a Top Priority for 2016," *Forbes*, December 6, 2015, https://www.forbes.com/sites/joshbersin/2015/12/06/why-diversity-and-inclusion-will-be-a-top-priority-for-2016/?sh=5b608aa32ed5.

10. David Rock and Heidi Grant, "Why Diverse Teams Are Smarter," *Harvard Business Review* digital articles, November 4, 2016, https://hbr.org/2016/11/why-diverse-teams-are-smarter.

11. Mursal Hedayat, "Diversity in the Workplace Is Now More Critical Than Ever," *Forbes*, June 24, 2020, https://www.forbes.com/sites/mursalhedayat/2020/06/24/diversity-in-the-workplace-is-now-more-critical-than-ever/?sh=17b015ad60aa.

12. Sylvia Ann Hewlett, Melinda Marshall, and Laura Sherbin, "How Diversity Can Drive Innovation," *Harvard Business Review*, December 2013.

13. David A. Thomas, "Diversity as Strategy," *Harvard Business Review*, September 2004.

14. Accenture, AAPD, and Disability:IN, "Getting to Equal: The Disability Inclusion Advantage," 2018, https://www.accenture.com/_acnmedia/pdf-89/accenture-disability-inclusion-research-report.pdf.

15. Corinne Post, Boris Lokshin, and Christophe Boone, "Research: Adding Women to the C-Suite Changes How Companies Think," *Harvard Business Review* digital articles, April 6, 2021, https://hbr.org/2021/04/research-adding-women-to-the-c-suite-changes-how-companies-think.

16. Hewlett, Marshall, and Sherbin, "How Diversity Can Drive Innovation"; Rocio Lorenzo and Martin Reeves, "How and Where Diversity Drives Financial Performance," *Harvard Business Review* digital article, January 30, 2018, https://hbr.org/2018/01/how-and-where-diversity-drives-financial-performance.

17. Rock and Grant, "Why Diverse Teams Are Smarter"; Katherine W. Phillips, Katie A. Liljenquist, and Margaret A. Neale, "Is the Pain Worth the Gain? The Advantages and Liabilities of Agreeing with Socially Distinct Newcomers," *Personality and Social Psychology Bulletin* 35, no. 3 (2009): 336–350.

18. Erik Larson, "New Research: Diversity + Inclusion = Better Decision Making at Work," *Forbes*, September 21, 2017, https://www.forbes.com/sites/eriklarson/2017/09/21/new-research-diversity-inclusion-better-decision-making-at-work/?sh=2b18fba94cbf.

19. Alexa A. Perryman, Guy D. Fernando, and Arindam Tripathy, "Do Gender Differences Persist? An Examination of Gender Diversity on Firm Performance, Risk, and Executive Compensation," *Journal of Business Research* 69, no. 2 (February 2016): 579–586; Corinne Post, Boris Lokshin, and Christophe Boone, "What Changes after Women Enter Top Management Teams? A Gender-Based Model of Strategic Renewal," *Academy of Management Journal* 65, no. 1 (February 16, 2022), https://doi.org/10.5465/amj.2018.1039.

20. Paul Gompers and Silpa Kovvali, "The Other Diversity Dividend," *Harvard Business Review*, July–August 2018; "Yes, Investors Care about Gender Diversity," Kellogg Insight, March 2, 2020, https://insight.kellogg.northwestern.edu/article/women-in-tech-finance-gender-diversity-investors; Catalyst, "The Bottom Line: Connecting Corporate Performance and Gender Diversity," 2004, https://www.catalyst.org/wp-content/uploads/2019/01/The_Bottom_Line_Connecting_Corporate_Performance_and_Gender_Diversity.pdf.

21. Stephen Scott and Amy Edmondson, "Unlocking Diversity's Promise: Psychological Safety, Trust and Inclusion," *Reuters*, April 13, 2021, https://www.reuters.com/article/bc-finreg-unlocking-diversity-inclusion/unlocking-diversitys-promise-psychological-safety-trust-and-inclusion-idUSKBN2C01N2.

22. McKinsey & Company, "Diversity Wins: Inclusion Matters," 2020, https://www.mckinsey.com/~/media/mckinsey/featured%20insights/diversity%20and%20inclusion/diversity%20wins%20how%20inclusion%20matters/diversity-wins-how-inclusion-matters-vf.pdf; American Sociological Association, "Diversity Linked to Increased Sales Revenue and Profits, More Customers," ScienceDaily, April 3, 2009, https://www.sciencedaily.com/releases/2009/03/090331091252.htm; Credit Suisse Research Institute, "The Credit Suisse Gender 3000 in 2021: Broadening the Diversity Discussion," 2021, file:///Users/dteppert/Downloads/csri-2021-gender-3000.pdf.

23. National Sexual Violence Resource Center, "False Reporting," 2012, https://www.nsvrc.org/sites/default/files/2012-03/Publications_NSVRC_Overview_False-Reporting.pdf.

24. Chai R. Feldblum and Victoria A. Lipnic, "Select Task Force on the Study of Harassment in the Workplace," US Equal Employment Opportunity Commission, June 2016, https://www.eeoc.gov/select-task-force-study-harassment-workplace#_Toc453686298; National Sexual Violence Resource Center, "False Reporting."

25. Feldblum and Lipnic, "Select Task Force on the Study of Harassment in the Workplace."

26. Tina Opie and Beth A. Livingston, *Shared Sisterhood: How to Take Collective Action for Racial and Gender Equity at Work* (Boston: Harvard Business Review Press, 2022).

27. Michael Housman and Dylan Minor, "Toxic Workers," HBS Working Paper No. 16-057 (Boston: Harvard Business School Publishing, 2015), https://www.hbs.edu/ris/Publication%20Files/16-057_d45c0b4f-fa19-49de-8f1b-4b12fe054fea.pdf.

28. Bresman and Edmondson, "Research."

29. Charles Duhigg, "What Google Learned from Its Quest to Build the Perfect Team," *New York Times Magazine*, February 25, 2016, https://www.nytimes.com/2016/02/28/magazine/what-google-learned-from-its-quest-to-build-the-perfect-team.html.

30. Julia Rozovksy, "The Five Keys to a Successful Google Team," re:Work, November 17, 2015, https://rework.withgoogle.com/blog/five-keys-to-a-successful-google-team/.

31. Bresman and Edmondson, "Research."

32. Workhuman, "How to Build Psychological Safety," July 2021, https://www.workhuman.com/resources/research-reports/how-to-build-psychological-safety.

33. Ruchika Tulshyan, "Why Is It So Hard to Speak Up at Work?," *New York Times*, March 15, 2021, https://www.nytimes.com/2021/03/15/us/workplace -psychological-safety.html.

34. Catalyst, "The Impact of Covid-19 on Workplace Inclusion: Survey," July 15, 2020, https://www.catalyst.org/research/workplace-inclusion-covid-19/.

35. Amy C. Edmonson, *The Fearless Organization: Creating Psychological Safety in the Workplace for Learning, Innovation, and Growth* (Hoboken, NJ: John Wiley & Sons, 2018).

36. Gitlab, "Psychological Safety," https://about.gitlab.com/handbook /leadership/emotional-intelligence/psychological-safety/#additional-resources.

37. Frances Frei and Anne Morriss, *Unleashed: The Unapologetic Leader's Guide to Empowering Everyone Around You* (Boston: Harvard Business Review Press, 2020).

38. Frei and Morriss, *Unleashed*.

39. Frei and Morriss, *Unleashed*.

40. Amy Elisa Jackson, "Why Salesforce's New Equality Chief Is Thinking Beyond Diversity," *Fast Company*, March 20, 2017, https://www.fastcompany .com/3069082/why-salesforces-new-equality-chief-is-thinking-beyond -diversity.

41. Rosalind Chow, "Don't Just Mentor Women and People of Color. Sponsor Them," *Harvard Business Review* digital article, June 30, 2021, https://hbr .org/2021/06/dont-just-mentor-women-and-people-of-color-sponsor-them.

42. Two books we find ourselves returning to for inspiration and wisdom on building a culture of inclusion are Lily Zheng's *DEI Deconstructed: Your No-Nonsense Guide to Doing the Work and Doing It Right* (Oakland, CA: Berrett-Koehler Publishers, 2022) and Ruchika Tulshyan's *Inclusion on Purpose: An Intersectional Approach to Creating a Culture of Belonging at Work* (Cambridge: MIT Press, 2022).

43. Francesca Gino et al., "Leaders Reflect on Diversity, Equity, and Inclusion," HBS Multimedia Courseware No. 923-701 (Boston: Harvard Business School Publishing, 2022).

44. Gino et al., "Leaders Reflect on Diversity, Equity, and Inclusion."

45. E. Annie Proulx, *The Shipping News* (New York: Scribner Classics, 1994).

46. We've learned an immeasurable amount from the great Byron Katie, who has pushed us to challenge *every* story, not just the primal ones. Katie's *Four Essential Questions* exercise brings you all the way to the point of liberation: Who would I be without this story?

47. Anne Morriss, Robin J. Ely, and Frances Frei, "Managing Yourself: Stop Holding Yourself Back," *Harvard Business Review*, January–February 2011.

CHAPTER 4

1. Howard Gardner, *Leading Minds: An Anatomy of Leadership* (New York: Basic Books, 1995), 41.

2. Richard Feloni, "The T-Mobile CEO Who Calls His Competition 'Dumb and Dumber' Explains How He Doubled Customers in 4 Years, and How a Group of Employees Made Him Cry," *Business Insider*, October 17, 2016, https://www.businessinsider.com/t-mobile-ceo-john-legere-company -culture-2016-10.

3. Merlijn Venus, Daan Stam, and Daan van Knippenberg, "Visions of Change as Visions of Continuity," *Academy of Management Journal* 62, no. 3 (June 2019): 667–690.

4. Valerie Strauss, "Harvard Business Dean Apologizes for Sexism on Campus," *Washington Post*, February 1, 2014, https://www.washingtonpost .com/news/answer-sheet/wp/2014/02/01/harvard-business-dean-apologizes -for-sexism-on-campus/.

5. "Our First Steps Forward," Riot Games press release, August 29, 2018, https://www.riotgames.com/en/who-we-are/our-first-steps-forward.

6. Keach Hagey et al., "Facebook's Pushback: Stem the Leaks, Spin the Politics, Don't Say Sorry," *Wall Street Journal*, December 29, 2021.

7. Emma Barker, "What the Facebook Whistleblower Did to the Company's Stock in 6 Weeks," *Time*, October 25, 2021, https://time.com/6104351/facebook -stock-whistleblower/.

8. Our colleague Rosabeth Moss Kanter has been writing and thinking about change leadership for decades. Any contribution we are hereby making with this book builds directly on her insight and scholarship.

9. Jeff Haden, "10 Years Ago, 'Cardboard' Pizza Almost Killed Domino's. Then, Domino's Did Something Brilliant," *Inc.,* January 14, 2021, https://www .inc.com/jeff-haden/10-years-ago-cardboard-pizza-almost-killed-dominos -then-dominos-did-something-brilliant.html.

10. Haden, "10 Years Ago, 'Cardboard' Pizza Almost Killed Domino's."

11. Matt Higgins has written a tour de force of this concept in his best-selling book *Burn the Boats: Toss Plan B Overboard and Unleash Your Full Potential* (New York: William Morrow, 2023).

12. Martin Neubert, "Ørsted's Renewable-Energy Transformation," interview by Christer Tryggestad, McKinsey, July 10, 2020.

13. Ørsted, "A Business Plan for Green Transformation," online advertisement hosted by *The Guardian*, https://www.theguardian.com/advertiser-content /orsted/a-business-plan-for-green-transformation, accessed December 2022.

14. Justin Bariso, "Amazon Has a Secret Weapon Known as 'Working Backwards'—and It Will Transform the Way You Work," *Inc.*, December 16, 2019, https://www.inc.com/justin-bariso/amazon-uses-a-secret-process-for-launching -new-ideas-and-it-can-transform-way-you-work.html.

15. Ryan Pendell, "6 Scary Numbers for Your Organization's C-Suite," *Gallup Workplace*, October 30, 2018, https://www.gallup.com/workplace/244100 /scary-numbers-organization-suite.aspx.

16. Mary Catherine Bateson, *Peripheral Visions: Learning along the Way*, 1st ed. (New York: HarperCollins Publishers, 1994), 10.

17. "Barrier-Breaking CEO Ursula Burns Offers Her Advice about What People Need from Leaders Now," California Conference for Women, https:// www.caconferenceforwomen.org/barrier-breaking-ceo-ursula-burns-offers -her-advice-about-what-people-need-from-leaders-now/.

18. "Barrier-Breaking CEO Ursula Burns Offers Her Advice."

19. Jan Carlzon, *Moments of Truth* (Cambridge, MA: Ballinger, 1987).

20. Margherita Beale, "A Fast-Selling Line of Pantry Staples Is Helping Momofuku Survive the Pandemic—and Figure Out the Future of Restaurants," *Forbes*, December 12, 2020, https://www.forbes.com/sites/margheritabeale /2020/12/12/a-sold-out-line-of-pantry-staples-is-helping-momofuku-survive -the-pandemic-and-figure-out-the-future-of-restaurants/?sh=54c50a0b2683.

21. Elizabeth G. Dunn, "Momofuku's Secret Sauce: A 30-Year-Old C.E.O.," *New York Times*, August 16, 2019, https://www.nytimes.com/2019/08/16 /business/momofuku-ceo-marguerite-mariscal.html#:~:text=Marguerite%20 Zabar%20Mariscal%2C%20who%20started,they%20expand%20a%20 restaurant%20empire.

22. Bryce Hoffman, "Have a Plan, Keep It Simple—and Stick to It," *Forbes*, March 31, 2015, https://www.forbes.com/sites/brycehoffman/2015/03/31/have -a-plan-keep-it-simple-and-stick-to-it/?sh=1bc0ab0248ff.

23. Tsedal Neeley and Paul Leonardi, "Effective Managers Say the Same Thing Twice (or More)," *Harvard Business Review*, May 2011.

24. Dharmesh Shah, "The Remarkable Power of Repeating Your Mission and Culture," ThinkGrowth.org, March 5, 2018, https://thinkgrowth.org/the -remarkable-power-of-repeating-your-mission-and-culture-984f7cc65acb.

25. Marguerite Ward, "Why Pepsico CEO Indra Nooyi Writes Letters to Her Employees' Parents," CNBC, February 1, 2017, https://www.cnbc.com/2017 /02/01/why-pepsico-ceo-indra-nooyi-writes-letters-to-her-employees-parents .html#:~:text=The%20letters%20make%20her%20employees,employee's%20 view%20of%20their%20company.

26. Daniel Goleman, Richard Boyatzis, and Annie McKee, "Primal Leadership: The Hidden Driver of Great Performance," *Harvard Business Review*, December 2001.

27. Brooks Holtom, Amy C. Edmondson, and David Niu, "5 Tips for Communicating with Employees during a Crisis" *Harvard Business Review* digital article, July 9, 2020, https://hbr.org/2020/07/5-tips-for-communicating -with-employees-during-a-crisis.

28. We've been deeply influenced by our colleague Robin Ely's work on the price *everyone* pays in a system with strict gender rules and boundaries.

29. Youngme Moon, Frances Frei, and F. Katelynn Boland, "Bringing Ideas to Life: The Story of Paul English," HBS No. 9-322-709 (Boston: Harvard Business School Publishing, 2022).

30. Ginni Rometty, *Good Power: Leading Positive Change in Our Lives, Work, and World* (Boston: Harvard Business Review Press, 2023).

31. Adia Harvey Wingfield, "Are Some Emotions Marked 'Whites Only'? Racialized Feeling Rules in Professional Workplaces," *Social Problems* 57, no. 2 (May 2010): 251–268.

32. Francesca Gino and Jeffrey Huizinga. "Steve Kerr: Coaching the Golden State Warriors to Joy, Compassion, Competition, and Mindfulness," Case 921– 001 (Boston: Harvard Business School Case, July 2020).

33. Nancy Koehn, *Forged in Crisis: The Making of Five Courageous Leaders* (New York: Scribner, 2017), 13.

CHAPTER 5

1. Taylor Branch, *At Canaan's Edge: America in the King Years, 1965–68* (New York: Simon & Schuster, 2007).

2. Martin Luther King Jr., "Beyond Vietnam: A Time to Break Silence," speech given at Riverside Church, New York, NY, April 4, 1967.

3. Valle's leadership helped to land the company on *Newsweek*'s "Best Places to Work" list, two years in a row, with a shout-out to the company's DEI efforts.

4. Amazon, "2016 Letter to Shareholders," April 17, 2017, https://www .aboutamazon.com/news/company-news/2016-letter-to-shareholders.

5. Ralph Waldo Emerson, *Prudence* (New York and San Francisco: Morgan Shepard Company, 1906), 21.

6. If you find yourself resisting this essential truth about excellence, we'll refer you to the first chapter of *Uncommon Service*: "You Can't Be Good at Everything" (Boston: Harvard Business Review Press, 2012).

7. Frances Frei and Anne Morriss, *Unleashed: The Unapologetic Leader's Guide to Empowering Everyone Around You* (Boston: Harvard Business Review Press, 2020).

8. This is a great summary from the First Round Capital team: "The 6 Decision-Making Frameworks That Help Startup Leaders Tackle Tough Calls," *The Review* (blog), https://review.firstround.com/the-6-decision-making -frameworks-that-help-startup-leaders-tackle-tough-calls.

9. Sandra J. Sucher and Stacy McManus, "Ritz-Carlton Hotel Company, The." HBS Case 601-163 (Boston: Harvard Business School Publishing, 2001).

10. Don Yaeger, "Part II: Ritz Carlton's Schulze on Empowering Employees to Think Like Owners," *Chief Executive*, December 7, 2022, https://chiefexecutive.net /part-ii-ritz-carltons-schulze-on-empowering-employees-to-think-like-owners/.

11. Yaeger, "Part II: Ritz Carlton's Schulze."

12. Micah Solomon, "Heroic Customer Service: When Ritz-Carlton Saved Thomas the Tank Engine," *Forbes*, January 15, 2015, https://www.forbes.com /sites/micahsolomon/2015/01/15/the-amazing-true-story-of-the-hotel-that-saved -thomas-the-tank-engine/?sh=26859f8b230e.

13. Allan Lee, Sara Willis, and Amy Wei Tan, "When Empowering Employees Works, and When It Doesn't," *Harvard Business Review* digital article, March 2, 2018.

14. Frances Frei and Anne Morriss, *Uncommon Service: How to Win by Putting Customers at the Core of Your Business* (Boston: Harvard Business Review Press, 2012).

15. Alison Sider, "How Southwest Airlines Melted Down," *Wall Street Journal,* December 28, 2022, https://www.wsj.com/articles/southwest-airlines -melting-down-flights-cancelled-11672257523.

16. James L. Heskett, "Southwest Airlines 2002: An Industry Under Siege," Case 9-803-133 (Boston: Harvard Business School, 2003); and Frances Frei and Corey B. Hajim, "Rapid Rewards at Southwest Airlines," Case 602-065 (Boston: Harvard Business School, September 2001, revised August 2004).

17. We originally heard this story from the great Earl Sasser, Baker Foundation Professor at Harvard Business School, in December 2006. It is retold in more detail in Frei and Morriss, *Uncommon Service*.

18. Michael Basch, *Customer Culture: How FedEx and Other Great Companies Put the Customer First Every Day* (Upper Saddle River, NJ: Prentice Hall PTR, 2003), 8.

19. Basch, *Customer Culture*.

20. Edgar H. Schein, *Organizational Culture and Leadership* (San Francisco: Jossey-Bass, 1991).

21. Dave Barry, *Dave Barry Turns Fifty* (New York: Ballantine Books, 1999), 181.

22. Microsoft, "Hybrid Work Is Just Work. Are We Doing It Wrong?" Work Trend Index Special Report, September 22, 2022, https://www.microsoft.com/en-us/worklab/work-trend-index/hybrid-work-is-just-work; Dialpad, "The State of Video Conferencing 2022," *Dialpad* (blog), dialpad.com/blog/video-conferencing-report/.

23. Korn Ferry, "Working or Wasting Time?" *Korn Ferry* (blog), November 13, 2019, https://www.kornferry.com/about-us/press/working-or-wasting-time]; Doodle, "The Doodle State of Meetings Report 2019," 2019, https://assets.ctfassets.net/p24lh3qexxeo/axrPjsBSD1bLp2HYEqoij/d2f08c2aaf5a6ed80ee53b5ad7631494/Meeting_Report_2019.pdf.

24. Claire Hughes Johnson, *Scaling People: Tactics for Management and Company Building* (San Francisco: Stripe Press, 2023), 382–390.

25. Frances Frei and Anne Morriss, *Fixable*, April 30, 2023, podcast, TED Audio Collective, https://www.ted.com/podcasts/fixable.

26. Frei and Morriss, *Fixable*.

27. Adam Bryant, "How to Run a More Effective Meeting," *New York Times*, https://www.nytimes.com/guides/business/how-to-run-an-effective-meeting.

28. Priya Parker, "Find Your Lighthouses," *The Art of Gathering* (blog), October 27, 2021, https://mailchi.mp/priyaparker/a-hosting-game-changer?e=7a0653eaa8.

29. Priya Parker, *The Art of Gathering: How We Meet and Why It Matters* (New York: Riverhead Books, 2018), 3.

30. J. D. C. Little, "A Proof for the Queuing Formula: L = a?W," *Operations Research* 9, no. 3 (1961): 383–387.

31. Phil Wahba, "Crafting a Comeback at Etsy," *Fortune*, July 25, 2019, https://fortune.com/2019/07/25/etsy-ecommerce-growth-strategies/.

32. Wahba, "Crafting a Comeback at Etsy."

33. David Gelles, "Inside the Revolution at Etsy," *New York Times*, November 25, 2017, https://www.nytimes.com/2017/11/25/business/etsy-josh-silverman.html.

34. Gelles, "Inside the Revolution at Etsy."

35. Mike Beedle et al., "Manifesto for Agile Software Development," http://agilemanifesto.org.

36. Amy C. Edmondson and Ranjay Gulati, "Agility Hacks," *Harvard Business Review*, November–December 2021.

37. We also encourage you to read Eric Reiss's *The Lean Startup* (New York: Crown Business, 2011), regardless of your company's stage. Reiss's work demonstrates the power of a minimum viable product (MVP) mindset, even if you're not in the software business.

38. Edmondson and Gulati, "Agility Hacks."

39. Edmondson and Gulati, "Agility Hacks."

40. Francesca Gino, "Managing a Polarized Workforce," *Harvard Business Review*, March–April 2022.

41. Liane Davey, "An Exercise to Help Your Team Feel More Comfortable with Conflict," *Harvard Business Review* digital article, March 14, 2019, https://hbr.org/2019/03/an-exercise-to-help-your-team-feel-more-comfortable-with-conflict.

42. Kerry Patterson, Joseph Grenny, Ron McMillan, and Al Switzler, *Crucial Conversations: Tools for Talking When Stakes Are High* (New York: McGraw-Hill, 2002).

43. Kim Scott followed *Radical Candor: How to Get What You Want by Saying What You Mean* (New York: St. Martin's Press, 2017) with *Just Work: How to Root Out Bias, Prejudice, and Bullying to Build a Kick-Ass Culture of Inclusivity* (New York: St. Martin's Publishing Group, 2021), where she explores the power of *all of us* working on behalf of *each of us*.

44. Chris Argyris, "Making the Undiscussable and Its Undiscussability Discussable," *Public Administration Review* 40, no. 3 (1980): 205–213.

45. Jeff Weiss and Jonathan Hughes, "Want Collaboration? Accept—and Actively Manage—Conflict," *Harvard Business Review*, March 2005.

46. Erin Meyer, "When Culture Doesn't Translate," *Harvard Business Review*, October 2015.

47. Matt Trombley, "The Beauty and Complexity of Finding Common Ground," speech given at TED Conference, June 2020.

48. Atif Masood Chaudhry and Rehman Asif, "Organizational Conflict and Conflict Management: A Synthesis of Literature," *Journal of Business and Management Research* 9 (2015): 238–244.

49. Karen A. Jehn and Elizabeth A. Mannix, "The Dynamic Nature of Conflict: A Longitudinal Study of Intragroup Conflict and Group Performance," *Academy of Management Journal* 44, no. 2 (April 2001): 238–251.

50. Linda A. Hill et al., *Collective Genius: The Art and Practice of Leading Innovation* (Boston: Harvard Business Review Press, 2014).

51. Amanda Ripley, "These Radically Simple Changes Helped Lawmakers Actually Get Things Done," editorial, *Washington Post,* February 9, 2023, https://www.washingtonpost.com/opinions/2023/02/09/house-modernization-committee-bipartisan-collaboration-lessons/.

52. Chris Cioffi, "They Tried to Modernize Congress. Now Time Is Running Out," *Roll Call*, September 13, 2022, https://rollcall.com/2022/09/13/tried-to-modernize-congress-now-time-running-out/.

53. Ripley, "These Radically Simple Changes."

CONCLUSION

1. Jim Loehr and Tony Schwartz, "The Making of the Corporate Athlete," *Harvard Business Review*, January 2001.

2. Arianna Huffington, *Thrive: The Third Metric to Redefining Success and Creating a Life of Well-Being, Wisdom, and Wonder* (New York: Harmony Books, 2014).

3. Tricia Hersey, *Rest Is Resistance: A Manifesto* (New York: Little Brown, Spark, 2022).

4. Mary Oliver, "Have You Ever Tried to Enter the Long Black Branches?" *West Wind: Poems and Prose Poems* (Boston: Mariner Books, 1998), 61.

INDEX

DISCLOSURES

Many of the insights and examples we use are derived from our experiences working with specific organizations. Both individually and in association with firms we have founded, including The Morriss Group, we have actively advised many of the companies in this book, including Uber, Riot Games, and WeWork. In addition, Frances has taught extensively in Harvard Business School's Executive Education program and in private executive education settings where she has engaged with leaders from many of the companies we discuss. Finally, some of the companies we mention are clients of The Leadership Consortium (TLC), an organization we started and where Anne currently serves as executive founder. These firms have sent high-potential leaders through TLC's Leaders Program, which is focused primarily on helping women and people of color prepare for senior leadership roles.

ACKNOWLEDGMENTS

First, thank you to our readers, who chose to suspend disbelief and indulge a premise that seems absurd on its surface: that hard problems can be solved quickly and sometimes with a single, brave conversation. We hope we've honored your leap of faith. And to those of you who made it this far and are taking the time to read these sentences, know that we see you as a special kind of book warrior.

We are deeply grateful for the talent and hard work of Dana Teppert, our intrepid research partner. Although her official title is Senior Researcher, a more accurate description would be Senior Research Magician or Senior Research Genius. Dana made this book better in countless ways.

We also want to thank Natasha Carr, our chief collaborator in turning ambitious ideas into things that have a chance of actually happening in the world. Those "things" include but are in no way limited to this book. Without Natasha, the world would get very little of us.

The outstanding team at Harvard Business Review Press believed in this book from the beginning. We are particularly grateful to Melinda Merino, our incredible editor, who has been a fantastic partner and champion of these ideas, even when we disappeared to solve problems for, um, more than a week. We hereby acknowledge that we pushed the limits of moving fast and fixing things.

Our early readers and thought partners made a significant contribution to this book. They include Emmy Berning, Drew Dixon, Hilary Frei, Corey Hajim, Claire Hughes Johnson, Sonia Nijhawan Mehra, Megan McTiernan, Lexi Reese, Cara Shortsleeve, and Thomas Wedell-Wedellsborg. It's thrilling to write these formidable names in a single sentence, and we'll simply offer that there's nothing this army of thinkers and changemakers can't do.

Our friends and colleagues at Harvard Business School have been on this adventure with us for decades, both personally and professionally. We are particularly thankful for the friendship, leadership, and intellectual courage of Ryan Buell, Amy Edmondson, Caroline Elkins, Hise Gibson, Francesca Gino, Karim Lakhani, Youngme Moon, Das Naryandas, and Tsedal Neeley. Where possible, we have tried to honor the way their ideas have shaped us—an impossible task, given their irrepressible influence.

We are grateful to our beloved sons, Alec and Ben, who cheered us on throughout the writing of this book. We love you, always, without bounds or conditions. We share the privilege of raising our children with wonderful people who make it possible for us to be parents and also active in the world. Angella Ramkhelawan and Kimberly Wick, we could not do any of this without you.

Finally, to all of the extraordinary fixers who have taught us what we know, only some of whom made it onto these pages. Thank you for your courage, wisdom, and willingness to share your leadership path with us. It turns out there's nowhere we'd rather be.

ABOUT THE AUTHORS

Frances Frei is a professor at Harvard Business School. Her research investigates how leaders create the context for organizations and individuals to thrive by designing for excellence in strategy, operations, and culture. Frances regularly works with companies embarking on large-scale change and organizational transformation, including embracing diversity and inclusion as a lever for improved performance. In 2017, she served as Uber's first senior vice president of leadership and strategy to help the company navigate its very public crisis in leadership and culture.

Anne Morriss is an entrepreneur, leadership coach, and founder of The Leadership Consortium, a first-of-its-kind leadership accelerator that works to help women and people of color prepare for senior leadership roles. She has spent the last twenty years building and leading mission-driven enterprises. Anne has worked with organizations and governments around the world on leadership, culture, and transformational change. Her collaborators have ranged from early-stage tech founders to public-sector leaders working to build national competitiveness.

Anne and Frances are also the authors of *Uncommon Service: How to Win by Putting Customers at the Core of Your Business* and *Unleashed: The Unapologetic Leader's Guide to Empowering Everyone Around You.* They are hosts of *Fixable,* a leadership advice podcast from the TED Audio Collective, and are recognized by Thinkers50 as among the world's most influential business thinkers.

You can learn more about their work at anneandfrances.com.